Local Radio Journalism

Local Radio Journalism

Second Edition

Paul Chantler and Sim Harris

87478

Focal Press
An imprint of Butterworth-Heinemann
Linacre House, Jordan Hill, Oxford OX2 8DP
A division of Reed Educational and Professional Publishing Ltd

A member of the Reed Elsevier plc group

OXFORD   BOSTON   JOHANNESBURG
MELBOURNE   NEW DELHI   SINGAPORE

First edition 1992
Reprinted 1994
Second edition 1997

British Library Cataloguing in Publication Data
A catalogue record for this book is available from the British Library

ISBN 0 2405 1422 X

Library of Congress Cataloguing in Publication Data
A catalogue record for this book is available from the Library of Congress

Printed and bound in Great Britain by
Hartnolls Limited, Bodmin, Cornwall

Contents

Acknowledgements

We are very grateful to the following people and organisations who have helped in the preparation of the text and illustrations for this book:

Sir Peter Gibbings, Chairman, the Radio Authority; Tony Stoller, Chief Executive, The Radio Authority; Rob van Pooss, Mick Garrett and Don Scott at Essex Radio; Margaret Hyde at BBC Essex; Colin Mason at Choice FM; John Perkins of Independent Radio News; Angus Moorat at Metro Networks; Paul Robinson at Talk Radio; Michael Bukht at Classic FM; Mike Vince and Sheila Mallett at Chiltern Radio; BBC Radio Publicity; Ingrid Bardua for taking many of the photographs; and, of course, Margaret Riley at Focal Press.

Paul Chantler would particularly like to thank Langley Brown, former news editor of BBC Radio Medway in the 1970s, who was the personal inspiration for him becoming a radio journalist.

Foreword

The collection and dissemination of all types of news is a vast industry, and radio plays a very important part in it. For news is one of the key elements in building radio stations' relationship with their audiences. Particularly in commercial radio, local news connects the station to the area in which it is broadcasting and identifies itself with its listeners.

Since 1991 and the implementation of the Broadcasting Act 1990, commercial radio stations have not been required to broadcast news. Without exception though, each of the 180 or so services, from the large London stations to tiny 'community' services, includes some sort of news coverage in their output.

The first edition of this book was published four years ago and became a standard textbook for journalism and media students. It sold out. Written by two experienced broadcasters, Paul Chantler and Sim Harris, the second edition of this comprehensive handbook explains how to break into the industry and, once in, how to develop the skills required.

Journalism is a competitive and demanding profession. It requires integrity and accuracy if the results are to be worthy of the efforts made to seek out stories and report findings. Broadcast journalism, in particular, demands that facts are sacrosanct as, unlike newspapers, government legislation seeks to prevent opinion from colouring radio or television news output. The Radio Authority has a code which covers the broadcasting of news and current affairs. This code implements the Broadcasting Acts which require radio stations to be accurate and impartial in their coverage of news and related programmes. The BBC's staff must adhere to a handbook which has similar guidelines. This book usefully underlines the importance of impartiality and accuracy in the broadcast journalist.

Over the last five years the Radio Authority has been busy developing commercial radio and, as a result, at the time of writing, there are 70 or so new local radio stations and three new national stations broadcasting. In addition, in the early 1990s, the BBC introduced Radio 5, the news and sports channel. New technology, digital audio broadcasting, will make more effective use of the spectrum which, in turn, will enable further series to be broadcast. Consequently, there are now more opportunities to become a broadcast journalist than ever before and this book should be essential reading for all media students.

Sir Peter Gibbings
Chairman
The Radio Authority

Preface to the second edition

When television became popular in the 1950s, there were predictions that radio would die. Forty years on and radio is actually much more exciting and diverse than ever before. Local radio is growing at a fast rate with many areas of the UK now enjoying a wide choice of styles and formats, and millions of people now getting their daily 'fix' of news from radio.

This means that local radio offers a challenging career to journalists at all levels, from the well-resourced and established local newsrooms of BBC stations with a big commitment to speech radio to the small one-town commercial stations, staffed only by one person, broadcasting local news for a few hours every morning.

This book is a working manual for radio journalists. We hope that you will find it helpful whether you are seeking your first job or have many years experience in local radio. For the second edition, we have made many alterations and additions, not only to reflect more up-to-date techniques, but also to make the book more detailed and comprehensive, as well as more logical and easy to read.

Since the first edition was published in 1992, there have been many changes to the structure of both BBC and commercial local radio in Britain and these are described in an overview of the industry. We have re-written the technical chapter to take account of digital recording and editing processes as well as the increased use of computers in radio stations in general and newsrooms in particular.

There are also new sections on a local station's news agenda and the techniques of winning audiences through different presentation styles, including a look at audience research and measurement. The legal section has been revamped and updated with a more comprehensive guide to libel defences and more extensive hints and tips on court reporting for radio. There is a greater emphasis in the reporting section on the techniques of production such as wrapping and packaging. Our glossary, too, has been extensively overhauled with explanations of old and new radio jargon. Most of the photographs are new too.

There are many definitions of news. Two of our favourites are, 'That which is new, interesting and true' by Robert McLeish, esteemed author of *Radio Production* (Focal Press) and, 'Subjects I want to know about in a short amount of time' by US radio news consultant Rasa Kaye. All journalists working in local radio have to work hard to deal with the dilemma which says: 'People like local news, but not other people's local news.' The skills, tools and techniques to do this are what the second edition of *Local Radio Journalism* is really about.

Paul Chantler
Sim Harris

1

The structure of British local radio

Local radio in the UK is either BBC or commercial. The BBC stations are funded publicly through the television licence fee. These stations are controlled by the BBC and are speech-based, consisting of news and community information. The commercial stations rely on advertising and sponsorship revenue. They are run by independent companies regulated by the government-appointed Radio Authority. Many of these companies are now owned by large groups such as EMAP, GWR and Capital, and, in general, are music- and entertainment-led but with local news and information.

BBC local radio

BBC local radio is a talk-based service focusing on local news, current affairs, information, community debate and local sport.

There are 38 BBC local stations across England serving different and contrasting communities. Some, such as GMR in Manchester and WM in the West Midlands, cover large conurbations while others, such as Radio Cornwall and Radio Lincolnshire, are based in predominantly rural areas. Scotland, Wales and Northern Ireland have their own separate national radio services.

On average, BBC local radio's speech content has increased from about 50% in 1990 to 80% in 1997. Each station is on the air for an average 18 hours a day, typically from 6am to midnight.

Commercial radio

Commercial radio survives on advertising revenue. In order to attract advertising, a commercial station has to attract a large audience and cater to the largest potential market. Therefore most commercial stations play different sorts of pop music supplemented by local news and information.

There are more than 180 local or regional commercial radio stations in the UK, almost all of them operating 24 hours a day. The local stations range from big city stations such as Capital in London, Clyde in Glasgow and Metro in Newcastle to small stations in rural areas like Moray Firth in Inverness, KFM in Tunbridge Wells and Radio Ceredigion in Aberystwyth. The Radio Authority is also currently licensing a handful of regional stations which cover populations ranging in size from one million to three million and include stations such as Galaxy 101 in the South-West, Heart FM in the West Midlands and Century Radio in the North-West.

All commercial stations have different formats. Among the most popular are Contemporary Hit Radio (top 40 chart music), Gold (oldies from the 1960s and 1970s), Adult Contemporary (classic hits from the 1970s, 1980s and 1990s) and Dance (club and disco music). In London, there is a wider range of 19 stations with more diverse formats including Jazz FM (jazz music), Melody (easy listening) and Premier (Christian). London has two all-speech local stations in News Direct and LBC.

The Radio Authority regulates the industry by awarding licences, dealing with complaints and ensuring all stations adhere to their Promises of Performance – the detailed specification of content and style which form part of their licence.

A brief history of local radio

Local radio in the UK started in 1967 when the BBC opened Radio Leicester as an experiment. Before that, there had been regional programmes on national radio but no truly local stations.

The BBC retained its monopoly for six years until the first commercial station, LBC, opened in London in 1973. It was followed a few days later by Capital Radio. Throughout the 1970s and early 1980s, the number of BBC and commercial stations continued to grow throughout the UK.

All local stations were given both an AM and FM frequency but in the mid-eighties, commercial stations were encouraged to split transmissions, offering different programme services on their two frequencies. Many chose top 40 on FM and gold with more speech and information on AM.

Meanwhile, the BBC grew its local town-based stations into countywide operations. Thus Radio Medway became Radio Kent and Radio Brighton became Radio Sussex.

In the late 1980s and early 1990s, both commercial and BBC stations consolidated. Commercial stations, independently owned by local companies, were acquired by larger groups and some BBC stations combined to cover more than just one English county. When re-licensing the commercial sector, the Radio Authority introduced official Promises of Performance for each station to ensure local content and programming were maintained despite any change in ownership.

In the commercial sector, the battle for audiences became more fierce with programming and promotional techniques imported from the US and Australia where commercial radio was better established. Commercial radio now has about half the total radio audience against all BBC services, national and local. In BBC local radio, more talk and speech has led to stations carving a niche for themselves among a generally older audience.

Now local radio competes with national radio. In addition to the five national BBC stations (One FM, Radio Two, Radio Three, Radio Four and Radio Five Live), there are three national commercial stations (Classic FM, Virgin Radio and Talk Radio).

Despite the greater proliferation of stations, the total number of people listening to radio seems to stay the same. In order to compete with an ever-increasing choice, radio has to become more 'ear-catching' than ever. Localness and local news are essential tools for this task.

2

Working in local radio

Understanding radio

The first step to becoming a radio journalist is to understand the strengths of the medium and why it is so potent. You can use these strengths to produce powerful, memorable radio.

Why radio?

Research into people's perceptions of news shows that many think the sheer brevity of radio means it is the purest source of news available.

They perceive newspaper news as lagging behind radio and TV. The downmarket tabloids are seen simply as entertaining and titillating scandal sheets featuring more on TV and film stars than real news events; the broadsheet papers appear more concerned with detailed analysis and comment. Television too is thought of as a complex medium needing a great many people to make it work, with its ability to react fast to a news story sometimes hampered by technicalities.

By contrast, people listen to radio news when they need to know quickly what is going on. They realise that because radio news is so short, it has to concentrate simply on reporting the facts.

Speed and simplicity

Radio is probably at its best when it is 'live' or reacting to an event happening 'now'. Because there are relatively few technicalities, a news story can be on the air in seconds and updated as it develops. Radio works best with news stories which require a quick reaction. There is a flexibility which exists in no other media because comparatively few people are involved in the process.

Radio can simply be one person, an audio recorder and a telephone. There are no cameras, lights or production assistants. Usually, it is just one broadcaster and a microphone separating him or her from the listener. You should always strive to make use of radio's greatest assets – speed and simplicity.

Making pictures

Radio is the best medium to stimulate the imagination. The listener is always trying to imagine what he or she hears and what is being described. These pictures are emotional – such as the tearful voice of a mother appealing for information about her missing teenage daughter. Pictures on radio are not limited by the size of the screen; they are any size you wish.

Person-to-person

Radio is a very personal medium. The broadcaster is usually speaking directly to the listener. This is why it is so important to think of the audience as singular. When you talk on the radio, you are not broadcasting to the masses through a gigantic public address system. You are talking to one person in the way you would speak if you were holding a conversation over a cup of coffee or pint of beer.

Radio also allows the full emotions of the human voice to be heard, from laughter through anger and pain to compassion. The sound of a voice can convey far more than reported speech. This is because the *way* something is said is just as important as *what* is being said.

Localness

The biggest strength of broadcasting news on local radio is that it gives a station its sense of being truly local. Local radio stations aiming for a broad audience ignore news at their peril. In an increasingly competitive marketplace, news is one of the few things which makes a local station sound distinctive and 'close to you'.

News from 'around the corner' is often just as important to a listener than news from around the world, if not more so in many cases. However, there is a danger of becoming too local. Policy judgements have to be made about what is local and what is too parochial or parish pump. Local radio news bulletins are not audio versions of local newspapers; for reasons of space if nothing else. The judgement of how local is local is an important one. For example, a story about a cat up a tree is too parochial for all radio stations. The same story about a fire-fighter being killed while trying to rescue the cat is not only a good local story, it is almost certainly a national one as well.

What makes a good local broadcaster?

Working in radio is a very public job. We all have a good chance to hear how it is done whether we prefer Radio One, Classic FM, BBC World Service or the local commercial radio station.

But what qualities are managers seeking in their staff and freelancers?

It is essential that you should know what you want to do. The first letters to be rejected by radio stations usually start: 'I would be willing to do anything, including making the tea.' The writers of such letters believe they are increasing their chances of employment by showing versatility. In fact, people who are too dazzled by radio in general are unlikely to be much use in practice.

Apart from journalists, the other major on-air performers are the presenters. The term 'presenter' can cover all kinds of broadcasting from being a DJ on a fast-moving music show to reading the shipping forecast on Radio Four.

Qualities of a radio journalist

There has rarely been a better time to start in local radio. The industry is growing fast and the main problem facing many editors is finding sufficient staff and freelancers who can do the job. Note the words 'who can do the job'. There is no shortage of people who would like to do it. Sadly not all of them have abilities to match their ambition.

A competent radio journalist has to combine the traditional talents of the reporter with the newer skills. Traditional talents mean an ability to write clear, easily understood English, a knack of summarising complicated situations and – most important of all – a 'nose for news' or knowing what makes a good news story.

In addition, the radio journalist must feel at home with both old and new technical equipment and techniques. This means editing tape, hard disk editing, recording links and packages, reading self-op live bulletins on air and conducting interviews. If all these words mean nothing, do not worry. They are all explained later.

The good radio journalist is flexible, technically competent, capable of working under extreme time pressure and able to juggle dealing with a major disaster and a funny story in the same hour. Journalists must be able also to think well on their feet, perhaps recording an interview or writing details of a court case story literally a few seconds before it is due on air.

The quality of imagination in a local radio journalist does not mean the quality of making stories up, but having ideas of news stories and treatments as well as seeing newsworthy possibilities in unpromising places, like apparently endless council meeting minutes and agendas.

Starting out

There are some journalists in broadcasting who are never heard on the radio. They may be sub-editors working in big national newsrooms like the BBC's General News Service which serves BBC local radio or Independent Radio News which serves many commercial radio stations. Such people are usually highly experienced; their jobs are rarely offered to newcomers.

The novice journalist starting out in radio is more likely to find a job at a local station. That means a smaller station where everybody has a go at everything. The news editor may well read the news and report and, during part of the day, the news staff may be reduced to just one person. Weekend shifts, if they happen at all, are frequently handled by one person doing everything from presenting bulletins to making hourly check calls and grabbing an interview or two for Monday morning between times.

There is one phrase that should never be heard in small local radio newsrooms: 'that isn't my job.' The versatility of a radio journalist is most full stretched at a local station. In dozens of small newsrooms, there are no specialists concentrating on just one type of subject like industry or politics, there are no sub-editors and there may not even be a newsroom secretary.

Today's news is most often presented by journalists. The old style 'newsreader' still survives on BBC national radio and on the World Service. Under the traditional system, the newsreader provides the voice and the news is written by other people. On local radio, the bulletins are usually presented by the reporting staff although some big commercial radio groups have experimented with one reader pre-recording separate bulletins for a number of stations, prepared by separate teams of journalists, from a central source which are then played out simultaneously. This system, though, is the exception to the rule.

There is one more quality not yet mentioned – at least not specifically. It is the most important quality of all in a radio journalist. That quality is *enthusiasm.*

Make no mistake, the job can be hard. It may mean unpredictably long hours, especially when a big story breaks. It may be demanding and stressful, with split-second deadlines to meet every day. It may even be lonely as you keep a newsroom going on a boring Sunday afternoon. It will certainly be unsociable – someone has to work Christmas Day! However, it can also be very enjoyable and rewarding as you get back with the lead story just in time or present a 'hard' bulletin, full of good, breaking news stories. In other words, the job can be great fun and highly satisfying. It is what you make it.

Getting the job

There is no traditional way into radio journalism. It is highly competitive and persistence is essential. Although it is desirable to have a high level of education, it is by no means a necessity. However, some organisations recruit virtually all graduates. Others prefer experience over education.

The best advice for young people wanting to become radio journalists is to combine the highest level of education with as much work experience as possible. Remember the power of offering your services for free! Many newsrooms welcome work experience students as an extra pair of hands and, although you may find yourself doing menial tasks such as tape reclaiming, it is an invaluable opportunity to look and listen and find out how the great news machine works.

Remember also to listen to the radio. You can learn lots from simply hearing a variety of different styles of radio news from the national stations like BBC Radio Four and Talk Radio to your local commercial station. Listen especially well to the output of stations for which you hope to work. It is surprising how few budding young journalists do this.

Local newspapers

Experience of working on a local newspaper is still one of the best ways to get a job in local radio, although the writing techniques are different. People from local papers come to radio with a thorough grounding in the rudiments of journalism and, sometimes, invaluable local knowledge.

They are trained in law, public administration, typing and shorthand – all useful skills for the radio journalist. They also have experience in covering all sorts of stories ranging from flower shows to inquests. Accuracy and balance are second nature to these people, who also tend to know the difference between a police sergeant and a superintendent! Newspapers are also the best way to have developed that essential 'nose' for news.

Hospital radio

In the way that local newspapers provide a grounding in journalism skills, hospital radio stations give a good grounding in practical radio skills. Hospital stations broadcast on closed circuits to patients in hospitals and hospices. There are hundreds of them throughout the UK. It is voluntary work, with a chance to try everything from presentation to outside broadcasts, often learning as you go along with no formal training. There is also the gratification that you are performing a useful service for patients in hospital (see Figure 2.1).

Facilities and the quality of output vary from station to station. One of the best ways to get a job in professional radio is to have a potent combination of local paper and hospital radio experience. If your local hospital radio station does not have its own local news programme, why not offer to put one together?

Student radio

Many universities have campus radio stations either broadcasting on a closed loop system which can only be picked up in college grounds.

Figure 2.1 Hospital radio is often a way in for future full timers. But this picture at Hospital Tunbridge Wells shows listeners can also become broadcasters! *Courtesy of the Kent and Sussex Courier*

Similar to hospital radio in terms of the variable facilities and quality of output, student stations are targeted towards educated young adults who want to hear specific sorts of music, generally alternative and indie music. Student stations have the added advantage of having the resource support which universities can offer.

Some student stations also carry news about college life. Putting together bulletins of college news and doing interviews for broadcast on student radio is an excellent way of starting a demo tape of your expertise to help get a job in professional radio. Many student stations are developing a growing reputation for innovation, creativity and excellence in both speech and music-based programmes.

Restricted service stations

Restricted service licences (RSLs) are low-powered temporary radio services issued by the Radio Authority usually for a period of 28 days. RSLs are for a limited geographical coverage area, such as a town or up to two miles of a city. Since 1991, the Radio Authority has licensed more than 1,000 RSLs.

Numerous groups or individuals run services covering a variety of events or themes such as arts festivals, religious celebrations, school projects, carnivals, charity and sporting events. Many RSLs are used for trial services if a group wants to apply for a permanent commercial radio licence and wishes to demonstrate a level of community support. As long as applicants meet the Radio Authority guidelines, services can be as varied as imaginations allow. Needless to say, these RSLs provide invaluable experience in all aspects of practical broadcasting and journalism.

College courses

There are now an increasing number of college courses teaching broadcasting skills in general and journalism in particular. Again, there is a lot of competition for places. Courses fall into two main categories – postgraduate courses leading to a diploma or similar qualification, or three-year courses leading to a media studies or journalism degree. The latter combines studying radio with television and other media but both usually include short attachments with working radio stations.

Prospective students need to take care in choosing the best type of course. While many radio courses are practical and vocational, by no means all of them are. Some offer students opportunities to write and present programmes, others encourage students to analyse broadcasting policy and the history of its institutions in a social and cultural context.

There is some sneering in the radio industry as many of the three-year media courses sometimes tend to be more theoretical than practical. However, radio managements should remember that these courses are not simply training courses geared towards the needs of the industry. A media studies graduate learns not only *how* to do it but also ask awkward questions about *why* things are done in a certain way and *what other ways* there are of doing things.

The reality is that a media studies graduate or a postgraduate student with a diploma can usually offer a unique combination of skills and abilities including practical radio and journalism as well as a theoretical appreciation of news and its place in society.

BBC training schemes

The BBC advertises a number of trainee jobs which are directly linked to operational needs and therefore vary from year to year.

In the past, schemes have been run for local radio reporters but, as needs have changed, it has become necessary to offer training that is bi-media for both radio and television. One of the most recent schemes is the Regional Broadcast Trainee scheme.

When considering candidates for traineeships, the BBC puts a high premium on writing and communication skills and evidence of interest and commitment to broadcasting.

Freelancing

Because of the competition, it is often difficult to find a staff job after college, local papers, hospital radio or RSL experience. One answer is to offer your services as a freelance radio journalist. You have to be adaptable, mobile and confident in your own abilities. It is not the option for you if you crave security, but it can be lucrative.

Marketing yourself

Many jobs are advertised in the pages of newspapers like the *Guardian* and *Independent* and magazines like *Broadcast*, the *Radio Magazine* and *UK Press Gazette*. You can apply for these jobs directly. Alternatively, you can seek advice from the BBC Corporate Recruitment Department or write speculatively to radio stations throughout the UK. You will be surprised at just how many busy news editors decide to see someone for an informal chat on the strength of a good letter and tape.

Although there may be no immediate vacancies, you will be ahead of the rest if you make a good impression.

Your marketing pack needs to consist of a neatly-presented and well organised CV, a covering letter (sent to the news editor with his or her name spelt correctly!) and a demo tape. The demo tape should be a good-quality cassette of you reading a short news bulletin plus examples of the rest of your work such as an interesting interview or fascinating feature. It need be no longer than five minutes at most and is usually about three.

Target one or two specific news editors at first, and if you do not succeed at first, be persistent. After about a week or ten days, follow up your mailout with a phone call if you have heard nothing.

If you are seeking freelance work, make sure news editors hear from you regularly and know about your strengths. The idea is to ensure your name is on their list of people to call when they need freelance help. Remember that one job usually leads to others as you spread your own network of contacts.

Whatever you do, keep trying as persistence is an impressive journalistic skill. It also helps to try and go and see people simply to ask for feedback and advice.

3

News gathering

The newsroom structure

Newsrooms vary in size depending on the radio station. However, there is usually a similar structure of staff who do specific and necessary tasks (Figure 3.1 a and b).

Head of News or News Editor

This is the senior journalist in the newsroom reporting directly to the

Figure 3.1(a) The newsroom for commercial stations Essex FM and The Breeze at Southend-on-Sea. Note sports editor Roger Buxton (*left*) still likes to use a manual typewriter!

Figure 3.1(b) The busy newsroom at BBC Essex in Chelmsford

Programme Director in commercial radio or Managing Editor in the BBC who is editorially and managerially in charge. On some stations, the Head of News is involved in the day-to-day running of the newsdesk including some reporting and presenting. In others, he or she deals more with policy and administration.

Editorial jobs include:

- helping to decide the frequency and times of bulletins
- setting the overall editorial agenda and news policy
- being responsible for the detailed style and content of news output
- deciding the proportion of local to national news
- making sure stories are fair, accurate and legally safe
- deciding what stories should be covered and by whom
- dealing with complaints

Managerial jobs include:

- recruiting and motivating staff
- compiling work rotas
- preparing a budget and working within it
- booking freelancers
- arranging payments to agencies

- attending public relations functions
- training and coaching junior staff

Bulletin Editor

This is the duty journalist responsible for hourly supervision of the content and compilation of the bulletins. They will usually read the bulletins themselves and self-op the desk. Other duties include:

- intaking audio
- checking the latest from the emergency services – 'doing the calls'
- checking that cues and copy conform to style and editorial policy
- double checking the accuracy, fairness and legality of stories
- looking for follow-up stories and new angles
- re-writing and freshening stories
- allocating reporters to stories

Senior Journalist or News Producer

This journalist acts as Bulletin Editor when required but concentrates mainly on collecting and preparing news stories from interviewing to voicing and audio packaging. The difference between this job and the more junior reporter job described below is that seniors or producers are more often concerned with making policy decisions, generating stories and exploring angles than actually doing the reporting job, although barriers in many newsrooms tend to be blurred.

Reporters

The reporters are the 'fire-fighters' of the newsroom. They follow up stories, do interviews and report from the scene. Their main job is to collect audio or actuality, write copy and think up new angles. The qualifications for the job include knowing what makes a good story, accuracy, persistence, speed and 'thinking radio' – the best way to cover a story in sound.

One-journalist newsrooms

Smaller stations operate with one or two journalists combining all these jobs. This is the way many American radio stations operate and looks like the way forward for some low-cost UK commercial stations. The main attributes needed are a clear sense of priorities and good time-management skills. Setting up and running a small news operation is described in more detail later.

Bi-media journalists

In some BBC centres, especially in cities, journalists work for both the local radio station and the regional TV operation. They produce stories on a central computer system which can be accessed by both local radio and TV. In some centres, TV journalists on the scene produce separate reports for local radio. The cost-effective BBC is keen at multi-skilling its local journalists to be able to work in both TV and local radio and is introducing specialist training courses to make this possible.

National news suppliers

A local radio station would be unconvincing indeed without local news. Equally, its news output must acknowledge there is a wide world beyond 'our patch'. The provision of national and international news for local radio is undertaken by several specialist organisations.

During the day, many local stations mix national and international news from the agency with local news gathered on site. Overnights and at off-peak times, these stations take the live bulletin service offered by some agencies (see 'live bulletins' below).

Radio news agencies, like their counterparts in newspapers, provide national and international stories 24 hours a day as they break. Because radio is a medium of sound, its agencies must provide not only news copy but also appropriate audio or actuality. The technical implications are that stations must be linked to their national agencies by satellite or landline. News copy is fed either to newsroom printers or directly into a newsroom computer system. Audio is fed on a separate channel or line and either recorded on tape or downloaded onto a digital hard disk system.

BBC General News Service (GNS). GNS supplies news stories and actuality to BBC local radio stations by landline. It is based at BBC Broadcasting House in London and not available to any other network. GNS provides only copy and actuality for BBC local stations to mix bulletins and there are no live bulletins.

Independent Radio News (IRN). IRN was formed in 1973 at the start of commercial radio in the UK. The service is available by satellite to most commercial radio stations. It provides a comprehensive service of bulletins in 'kit' form for local mixing as well as a live bulletin service 24 hours a day. Local stations do not pay cash directly for the service; IRN is financed through the Newslink scheme where national commercials, sold by IRN, are played out on local stations next to morning news bulletins. This finances the cost of the service which returns a proportion of the profit to the local stations depending on the size of audience delivered. The television news company ITN is contracted by IRN to be the supplier of news and the news operation is based at ITN's London headquarters (Figure 3.2).

Figure 3.2 The newsroom at Independent Radio News (IRN) at Gray's Inn Road, London

Metro Networks. Metro specialises in supplying traffic and travel news to local radio stations but has now started to supply national and international news. It provides a live bulletin service only. Its only client for news in late 1996 was Virgin Radio, the national rock station, but it has plans to expand further. In America, where Metro Networks started, its operational 'hubs' in main cities provide a 'one-stop-shop' supplying customised local and national news, travel and weather for local stations.

Services for local radio stations provided by Network News and Reuters ceased in early 1996.

The local intake system

Local newsrooms receive a continuous stream of national and international news stories either on their printer or, in a digital newsroom, in the form of a menu on screen. Many computerised newsroom systems automatically sort incoming data into specific lists designated by editors to allow quick scanning of available stories. Audio feeds are sent out at various regular times each hour, for example IRN has a regular feed at 20 minutes to each hour. Of course, a fast-breaking story may mean that audio arrives outside these times. Most bulletin editors are familiar with the 'late feed' which arrives just a few minutes before the top-of-the-hour bulletin.

In a newsroom with analogue equipment, audio will be recorded on a dedicated tape recorder called a 'logger' attached to a simple electronic device which switches it on just before each piece of audio is sent. The audio, once on tape at the local end, can then be dubbed onto cart for broadcast. It is possible to take the audio straight onto cart as it is fed from the agency but the logger should still be running in case the first cart copy is missed (Figure 3.3).

BBC stations take automation one step further: a signal is fed just before each piece of audio which not only starts the logger but also starts a cart if one is inserted into the machine.

In a digital newsroom, the audio is automatically 'captured' by a sensing device and stored on the computer hard disk system. It appears in an on-screen menu of available audio and can then be edited, stored, moved and called up when needed for playout on air.

Figure 3.3 Journalist Annabel Fisher taking a cut from the IRN logger tape at Essex FM

Data feeds

The agencies provide much more in their data feeds than simple cues for audio. A typical hour will also produce some copy stories, at least one summary for headlines, financial news, entertainment news, music charts and perhaps a weather forecast. There will also be a variety of service messages; the feeds are used as a mailbox for the network and may carry all kinds of other information.

It is part of the Bulletin Editor's job to assess all this information either using it, passing it to someone else or throwing it away.

Live bulletins

IRN provides two- and three-minute bulletins every hour, 24 hours a day, read from London, which can be taken live by local stations. Some commercial stations use this and 'tag' their local news on the end. Others compile their own bulletins during the day, mixing local news with material sent from IRN. There is no equivalent service in the BBC.

Television audio

Some commercial stations are reaching agreements with local television companies to use TV audio in radio news bulletins. This allows them access to quality audio on big news stories without having to send a reporter to gather it. Access is usually permitted off air, i.e. by the radio station recording the output from the TV news programme. Depending on the agreement, the radio station may have to credit the TV company.

Sources of local news

News arrives in a local radio newsroom from many different sources:

- the emergency services
- press releases
- public utilities
- politicians and councils
- listeners
- colleagues
- pressure groups
- freelance journalists and agencies
- 'rivals'

When you have this information, you have to decide the answers to two key questions. First, is it reliable? Second, is it newsworthy? If the answer to both questions is 'yes', you have a story.

'No' to the first question will mean further checking. For example, a member of the public reports a serious road accident. You must verify it with the emergency services before using it as a story on air.

'No' to the second question is usually the end of the matter. However, always be alert to possible links with other stories. Never be afraid to test your decision on colleagues.

The emergency services

The police, fire, ambulance and coastguard services have a unique relationship with the media – both sides need the other. Information from these sources is often the staple diet of dramatic stories featured in local radio news bulletins. As publicly-funded organisations, the day-to-day work of the emergency services should be accountable. They often need to use the media to put over preventative messages about crime and safety as well as appealing for witnesses.

Regular check calls must be made to all the emergency services. Many now have voicebank systems where you can phone an unlisted number and hear an updated list of what has been happening recorded by a press officer. Sometimes, the emergency services will call you with tip-offs. Make sure you have met the press officers in each service and ensure that a good relationship continues. If you fall out (maybe a story was given to your rival station), make it your business to resume friendly relations as soon as possible.

Press officers are not the only sources of news stories. For example, a good local newsroom will not only make a point of speaking to the press office or listening to the voicebank recording regularly, but also talking direct to the operational officers on the ground and 'teasing' out some of the offbeat stories which occur (Figure 3.4).

A word of warning: the police do not always observe the laws of libel and contempt as well as they might. Treat all information from them with care and subject it to the same legal tests as you would any other story.

Press releases

Press releases are an excellent source of basic information but need to be looked at carefully. They are distributed by people who want you to express a story in their terms. In reality, what they want to say may not be a story – for example, shops putting out 'press statements' about winter sales. Alternatively, it may be genuine news but one-sided – for example, a release from a political party.

In most cases, you will need to contact the source of the release to verify facts, get more information or set up an interview (Figure 3.5).

Phoning people about their releases can be an education, particularly when public relations companies are involved. There are good, efficient PR companies who earn the fees they charge their clients by releasing factual, well-researched and well-angled information and make covering

Figure 3.4 A typical police control centre at Kent Police Headquarters, Maidstone. *Courtesy: Kent Police*

a story easier. There are also incompetent firms who waste time and money all round. Be particularly wary of any PR company sending out a press release to radio stations enclosing photographs (think about it!), referring to your 'readers', inviting you to a photocall, omitting phone numbers or forgetting to include the date of a forthcoming event.

NEWS FROM THE BUCKSHEE GROUP

For Immediate Release   31st August 1996

Buckshee Technologies Ltd, a member of Buckshee International plc, is to transfer the production of hydraulic components from its factory in Newtown to its principal plant in Highworth. This decision follows a review of the company's manufacturing facilities in the light of changes in defence procurement and the continuing need to reduce, wherever possible, operating costs.

The Newtown plant will be closed and the 315 employees will be leaving the company. The company much regrets making this reduction in personnel and will provide job and financial counselling to assist those affected in finding alternative employment.

Note to Editors: Buckshee Technologies Ltd comprises a group of companies supplying the servicing control systems and components for the international aerospace and defence industries.

Enquiries to: James Edwards, Head of Media Relations, on 01702 333 711.

Figure 3.5 Example of a press release from a company giving news of redundancies

When you do make contact, among the most idiotic responses are: 'Why do you want to talk to anyone? It's all in the press release...'; 'We could get someone to talk to you about this towards the end of next week,' and 'You won't actually want to record this, will you?'

However, if the release comes from an 'amateur' source, you can be more forgiving about errors. Local people like charities, pressure groups and religious organisations do not know the rules like you do.

Public utilities

The organisations which supply our electricity, gas, water and communications are all promising sources of news. Treat their press releases with caution as they will usually be 'slanted' towards the most positive angle.

As with the emergency services, ensure you are in touch with the relevant press officers. Make sure you have the names and numbers of local managers too, especially if the main press office is a long way away. Get to know them better by taking up invitations to visit the local telephone exchange, sewerage works or railway station. It takes some time, but it can be editorially rewarding – and there is usually some lunch laid on as well!

Politicians and councils

Your local MP will be a constant source of views and comment. Stay in touch with him or her but remember they have the benefit of a formidable party media machine behind them. MPs usually distribute scores of press releases and are always almost available for interview. In interviews, there are no-holds-barred because they should be expert media performers and able to cope with even the most rigorous questioning.

Local politicians or councillors are slightly different because their expertise varies widely. Some will be more effective than others. Do not overlook their usefulness when you want comments about a controversy. Know the difference between councillors and council officers. Councillors are elected members of the council and officers are salaried staff who make recommendations to members for decision. Both can be useful.

A constant source of local news is the tidal wave of agendas and minutes from councils, health authorities and other public bodies which usually flood into newsrooms. They are frequently tedious – but make sure you go through them, because a good story can lurk deep inside. Many minutes will reflect decisions already taken; agendas will preview recommendations. Remember it is perfectly proper to preview matters for decision by councillors on the day of the meeting. However, if you preview, you must follow up and report what actually happened the next day.

Listeners

All kinds of people can phone or wander in to a radio station with boring, rambling tales of rows with bosses or problems with noisy neighbours. Sometimes they bring a good story – but, if not, listen patiently and courteously. Even if they have wasted your time, it is good public relations to express sympathy and give them the address of the local Citizens' Advice Bureau. If you do follow up a story, remember not only to check the facts thoroughly but also that there are two sides to most stories and uncorroborated information should not be accepted at face value.

Tip-offs from listeners can be vital to get ahead on big breaking stories. For example, a listener phoning to tell you there is a big fire in his street can provide a good eyewitness account of what is happening. Many radio stations encourage listeners to phone in with tips. However, beware of hoaxers and ensure you get official confirmation of an incident before broadcast. It is a rare occasion where you will put something direct on air without checking.

Colleagues

It has been said – truly – that everyone working on a radio station should be a 'stringer' for the newsroom. Commercial radio station sales staff are out and about all day selling advertising, so encourage them to call you if they see or hear anything unusual. They are often the first to hear gossip about companies closing or expanding. Other staff, from the managing editor to the cleaners, can also come across stories by accident. Make sure they know you will be glad to listen.

Pressure groups

Pressure groups simply want to put their side of a story as often and as forcefully as possible. Do not let them libel anyone and do your best to balance their story with the other side's point of view.

Freelance journalists and agencies

A good relationship with local news agencies and freelance journalists is usually essential for a local newsroom. It would be impossible for most radio stations to cover legal proceedings in courts without copy supplied by them. Radio journalists do not have the time to sit in court all day nor necessarily the contacts to know which defendant is appearing where and when. Agencies and freelance reporters can also sometimes ferret out a story which has eluded you simply because they have better established contacts or have more time with which to work on a story. However, do not feel hurt and humiliated if a really good story finds its way to the national newspapers from a local agency – the big papers will pay hundreds of times the fee the agency can get from you.

Beware of agencies and freelance reporters who rewrite stories from the local press. Also watch agencies who rewrite press releases. This is easy money for them but a pointless payment for you. Find out why you did not receive the release; perhaps the sender was unaware of your existence.

'Rivals'

There is an attitude on some radio stations that rival stations are not worth listening to. This could be a mistake. It is your job to know what other stations – or TV shows or newspapers – are doing. Use them as a source of tip-offs but never 'lift' a story without checking it thoroughly first. Also try and find a different angle to give the story a fresher spin.

It is easy to become distracted with rivalry and going 'one-up' on other radio stations. Remember that very few people listen to two news bulletins on different stations at the same time; there is little to be gained by a one-on-one hour-on-hour battle over individual stories. The best a station can do is garner a general reputation for being 'first for news' or 'number one for news' over a period of time through a combination of effective on-air promotion and positioning.

Planning and developing stories

The newsroom is likely to represent the biggest area of 'input' into a radio station. Press releases, letters, phone calls, tip-offs, faxes and other information all arrives on the newsdesk. It is vital to have suitable systems in place to assess the importance of all this information quickly and either action it, pass it on to whoever needs it or file it away until it is needed.

The newsroom diary

The heart of a local newsroom is its diary. All information about events supplied in advance is written in the dairy under the appropriate date. Usually, these are A4 size hardbound book-style diaries but some newsrooms now have an 'electronic' diary as part of their computerised system with data available on screen.

It is up to everyone to put entries into the diary as soon as possible. One good system is that supporting papers such as the relevant council agenda, press release or letter are filed in the diary file – with numbers 1 to 31 corresponding to the days of the month. It should be the job of the reporter dealing with overnight stories (i.e. those for next morning) to look through the diary and diary file, and process previews of events happening the following day. On the day itself, it is the job of the Duty News Editor to assess what stories need covering given the resources available. In addition, a well-maintained 'futures' file with general cuttings and releases helps to generate ideas, especially on 'slow' news days when little is happening.

It is important that the newsroom is highly organised in its information flow and there is a tray or file allocated to receiving all this vital input from outside. This must be checked and processed regularly and not allowed to amass and overflow.

Newsdesk resource management

With the information from the diary at hand, decisions need to be made about how stories can best be covered. In some newsrooms, there are many staff and freelancers ready to be sent out on stories. Usually a newsroom conference is held to decide who does what, with what angle, and for when it is needed (Figure 3.6). In smaller newsrooms, it may simply be a case of deciding which story is worth following up by telephone by the one Duty Reporter.

The Duty Editor (which can be the Head of News/News Editor or a Producer/Senior Journalist) must always make allowances for the unexpected when planning coverage of the day's news. Reporters may be allocated to cover the opening of a new hospital wing, a Royal visit, a council press conference or a controversial public meeting, but it is important to leave some leeway so that dramatic, unforeseen events can be dealt with, such as an explosion or train crash. Reporters on the road should carry a bleeper, a mobile phone or, at the very least, make regular check calls back to base.

Remember, though, journalists cannot simply be re-active and wait for stories to happen; it is vital to be pro-active and chase their own stories through contacts gleaned through working on other stories in the past.

Developing stories

Reporters are allocated to specific stories. Each is briefed and given all the relevant background information from the diary file. It is the job of the Duty Editor to brief the reporter on the possible angles and ways of treating the story. Angles are the various ways a story can be told from different viewpoints. Treating the story means deciding whether the story becomes a copyline, interviews or package (see below). It is also important that each reporter is given a deadline so he or she knows exactly what is expected, by what time and in what form. There is no place or time in the newsroom for confusion.

Figure 3.6 The morning conference to decide the day's agenda at Essex FM

Newsroom contacts

A newsroom needs a system for quickly finding the name and phone number of anyone in the news. The best way to organise this is to create a contacts book – a simple A to Z index of people and organisations. Computerised newsrooms usually have an on-screen database version of this available to all.

It is a good rule that any phone number used by a journalist should be entered in the contacts file. This way a useful and comprehensive list of contacts is available speedily. It is important that the contacts, if written, are listed legibly, that everyone in the newsroom understands the system and what they have to do to find a number or put one in. For example, all police phone numbers – including those of the force press officer – should be listed under 'police' and not under the individuals concerned.

Many newsrooms have succeeded or failed by the quality of their collective contacts. In addition, journalists will inevitably develop their own databases of personal contacts who have been particularly helpful to them or may provide a useful source of stories in future. One good idea, on slow news days when dairy stories are hard to find, is to ring round these contacts simply to stay in touch. You will be surprised how often a casual chat with a contact can yield a good story.

Resisting pressure

There are innumerable outside pressures to which the radio newsroom is subjected.

Political parties regularly put pressure on newsrooms to present an item of news in the way they want, or accuse journalists of bias. For example, Labour supporters accuse newsrooms of Tory bias; Conservatives equally accuse newsrooms of Labour bias. If a speech by a representative of one party is given prominence, the next minute a voice on the phone complains of bias because equal prominence was not given to some speech by a member of another party, regardless of the fact it had no news value.

Commercial interests working through public relations companies try to slip in free advertising disguised as a news item. Usually such attempts are unsubtle in the extreme and easily detected. However, you should never be off your guard.

Listeners with personal axes to grind are another source of pressure. They are always ready to complain that we give too much or too little to this, that or the other.

People who want something kept quiet are another regular source of pressure. Usually, this is some kind of court case; the argument used is that to broadcast the item would cause suffering, upset or worry to relatives of the accused person, particularly if he or she turns out to be a person who occupies a position of standing in the community.

In all these cases, you must be bound by your sense of responsibility, fairness and independence. You must not bow to pressure.

Story treatment

Copy

The quickest way to cover a story is simply as 'copy' – that is, with no audio of any kind. Copy stories of one sentence or two are used for headlines; they are also a good way of giving a news bulletin pace and making it sound busy, with several stories following each other quickly. If a story has been running as audio but you are reluctant to drop it entirely, reduce it to copy. However, a bulletin of all copy sounds dull; it is no replacement for fresh, lively audio.

Interviews

The traditional way to cover a story for radio is to interview someone. Just who depends partly on you. You could, for example, decide to put a Labour accusation in the cue to a political story and have some interview audio from a Conservative denying it all – or the reverse.

Voicers

'Voicing' a story is another way of doing it. A voicer or voice-piece is less effective than an interview but sometimes the only way to improve on straight copy and used in many cases when there is too much information to get over in one piece of copy. In court cases, voicers are virtually standard; only rarely can you obtain audio about a court case – and almost never while the case is progressing because any comment could easily become contempt of court. Voicers are also used when a big story is breaking to put over the basics of a story (a 'holding voicer') while audio is gathered. The maximum duration of voicers varies from station to station; in general the BBC aims for between 35 and 40 seconds and commercial radio likes 25 to 30 seconds at the most.

Cuts, clips and soundbites

Cuts and clips are the same thing; a cut in commercial radio and a clip in the BBC are both short pieces of audio. More recently, cuts and clips have been called 'soundbites'. They could be part of an interview or an excerpt of audio recorded on location – anything from part of a speech to sounds of a riot. Good cuts have a proper start and a proper finish; they should not sound as if they have been taken from something longer. Again, acceptable duration is slightly longer at BBC stations – up to 40 seconds or so. Commercial stations like no more than 30 seconds maximum and, in many cases, considerably less. Some fast-moving pop stations take cuts of no more than 10 seconds to maintain the pace of a bulletin.

Wraps and packages

Once again, the words 'wrap' and 'package' both mean the same and are usually used in commercial radio and the BBC respectively. The wrap consists of at least one cut surrounded by a reporter's voice. It can be short – a single cut of 10 seconds inserted in 20 seconds of reporter's voice to make 30 seconds. Alternatively a wrap can run three minutes or more for use in a news programme. They are an excellent way of putting both sides of an argument. For example:

REPORTER: Angry parents lobbying County Hall this morning claimed that the increase in school meal prices will mean many children either starving or living on unhealthy chips. Eileen Duncan, ... whose three children go to St James' Middle School in Newtown, ... says she can't possibly afford more than ten pounds a week for their lunches alone.

CUT: DUNCAN / 22" / Out: '...absolute disgrace.'

REPORTER: But councillors on the education committee are defending the price rise. Conservative Ravi Singh says the meals are still to be subsidised at 72 pence a day.

CUT: SINGH / 25" / Out: '...see reason.'

And so on. The combination of scene-setting from the reporter and comment from people affected makes the story come alive. It would, of course, be even better with the sound of the demonstrators chanting slogans at the beginning.

Newsroom style guide

You will have noticed that the names of types of audio and durations vary between the BBC and commercial radio. In fact there are many more minor variations depending on the philosophy of individual editors and the style and format of station as well as the needs of the target audience. Almost every station develops its own 'house' style. For this reason, a style guide is helpful. It should set out the ground rules on durations, cue layout, audio labelling, writing style and news agenda together with many small details that everyone in the news team follows instinctively after a while. The style guide is an excellent point of reference if there is any uncertainty and makes life much easier for new staff or occasional freelancers working on shifts.

4

News writing

The business of radio is to communicate. If we fail to communicate, then we fail as radio journalists. Your aim must be intelligibility – *immediate* intelligibility. A carelessly-turned phrase, an ambiguity of expression, a complicated sentence and an illogical sequence of events are all fatal to news on radio. There is no room in a radio news bulletin for complexity, vagueness or obscurity. You must know what you want to say – and you must say it with directness, simplicity and precision.

Remember that dullness is a sin. No story should be regarded as routine. The way to capture the listener's interest is through your enthusiasm. If you take a jaded and apathetic attitude, it will produce a dull story. There is no reason to reduce every story to a flat recital of facts. Always be on the lookout for the detail that brings a story to life, such as the remark that reveals a personality or a phrase that makes a scene vivid.

Any news story can be written in a number of different ways. However, there are some basic tools and techniques which will help the journalist – and the listener.

Telling the story

Good news writing is the hallmark of good journalism. You can have the best story ever but if you cannot put it over in a way your listener understands, then you might as well not bother.

Writing for the radio should reflect that you are *telling* the story to someone, not making ministerial-like pronouncements. You are not 'broadcasting' to the masses; simply explaining to an individual what is going on.

You should write in a clear, crisp, concise, compelling and non-stuffy way. Your words should not be the words of the sensational tabloid newspapers, but you should not be afraid of using informal language when appropriate. A good story will almost write itself.

Remember, you are writing for the ear not the eye. You should write as you speak, in colloquial English, with short sentences and one thought per sentence. Always ask yourself, 'Would I say it that way myself?' or 'Do my friends talk like this in the pub?' For example, people actually say: 'There's a big fire at a shop in the town centre' not 'Fire-fighters wearing breathing apparatus have been fighting a massive blaze at a retail store.'!

Know what you want to say and say it conversationally in everyday language, but do not use slang or be slapdash. It takes skill and effort to write concise, lively copy on what may seem like a complicated or detailed story.

The aim is to write news for radio as natural conversation speech tempered with order and precision. The result is a style that is crisp, economical, direct and colloquial. It prefers the short word to the long one; the simple sentence to the complex; the concrete to the abstract; the active voice to the passive; and the direct statement to the inverted sentence.

Before you write a story from your notes or a press release, ask yourself: 'What is this story really about?' and 'What is it about this story that will *really* interest my listener?' It is sometimes helpful to read through your notes or the handout, put them to one side and then try and tell the story on paper without reference to the original source, apart from to check the facts. It is no longer a story from a news agency, press release or colleague. It is now *your* story. And you must tell the story as it appears to you.

Keep it short

The topline of your story must be short and snappy. It should hook the listener's attention and make him or her want to turn up the volume. At the same time, the topline should prepare the listener for the tale of a chain of events which are unfamiliar. Remember your listener may only be half listening, thinking about something else and about to switch off.

Do not make the mistake of trying to tell the whole story in the first line. Many newspapers do this but it does not work in radio. Give your first line impact. Then lead the listener through the story step-by-step and thought-by-thought, with each sentence elaborating on the previous one with a well-ordered narrative. Try writing one short sentence followed by a longer one as this helps increase the pace. As a rough guide, if you have a sentence that stretches to two lines on the computer screen, try and split it into two separate sentences.

Put one thought into each sentence and avoid pairs of commas with long sub-clauses in between. By the time you read the end of such a sentence, the listener will have forgotten what the start was all about.

Try not to start with the story's most important words. People do not hear individual words on the radio but pick up groups of words or phrases. Also try to keep the story fresh by rewriting the first line in two or three different ways. Be particularly careful about your choice of first word. Listeners often miss the first word as their attention is not fully engaged. It is therefore important not to begin your story with a key word or unfamiliar name. For example, 'Butter is to cost more' is a simple, direct statement. Unfortunately, some listeners will miss the first word and be left wondering what it is that will cost more. It is usually better to risk being slightly more long-winded and say 'The price of butter is going up.'

Keep it simple

All radio stories benefit from being kept simple. Try to think of word economy when writing. For example, 'A multiple pile-up on the M25 has left 15 people in hospital' rather than 'Thirteen cars, three lorries and a bus have collided between junctions 7 and 8 on the clockwise carriageway of the M25, leaving more than a dozen injured.'

Childlike simplicity is the essence of good radio writing. When you talk in the pub or over a cup of coffee, you usually talk in perfect radio style. For example, 'Rob's been taken to hospital . . .' 'Carol's husband has left her again . . .,' or 'that Robinson boy's in trouble again . . ..'

Write to make things easier to understand for your listener. For example, 'The council tax in Blanktown may go up again . . .' is far better than 'A meeting of the Blanktown Council finance committee last night heard that expenditure forecasts show an increase which may have to be passed on to householders.'

If you have information which your listener needs to be told, make sure you understand what he or she needs to know and why. For example,

'Blanktown Chamber of Commerce has agreed to provide low-cost public transport to the new retail park in Highfield' actually means 'There'll be cheap buses to the shops in Highfield.'

Keep it happening now

Radio's greatest strength is its immediacy. Therefore the use of the present tense, which gives the impression that something is 'happening now', is often appropriate, especially in the first line of stories.

Make sure you write in the present tense whenever possible. For example, 'Doctors have expressed surprise at the length of hospital waiting lists,' becomes 'Doctors say they're surprised at the length of hospital waiting lists.'

Always make the subject of a sentence 'active' rather than 'passive'. For example, 'Paul Hope fired a single shot at the police officer,' rather than 'The police officer was hit by a single shot fired by Paul Hope.'

Always think about how you can write about what is happening now. For example, 'A woman's in hospital after . . .', or 'A family's waiting at the hospital bedside of . . . .' However, beware that you should not give false impressions for the sake of this.

Keep adjectives to a minimum

Many journalists try to amplify their stories by using too many adjectives. This has the effect of simply annoying the listener. Sometimes adjectives are necessary but all too often they are over-the-top. Gimmicks and fancy words simply get in the way of the story. For example, "crucial relegation clash". How 'crucial' is it? Will the team get relegated if they lose, or will they just get into trouble at the bottom of the table? Using the word 'crucial' does not make this story any clearer. Make sure any adjectives you use give additional information.

Facts should be treated with the utmost respect. For example, if we do not know that a fire 'ripped' through a building, then we should not say so.

It is perfectly acceptable to add whatever 'colour' is available to a story. But if something did not happen in a certain way, you should not say it did simply to enliven your story. It is far better to have a factually correct story than a stunning couple of paragraphs which are exciting and racy but incorrect.

Language and grammar

There are a number of basic language rules designed to create better news writing. The list is not exhaustive and many newsroom style guides have their own favourites. Here are a few dos and don'ts:

- Do use *specific* words (such as 'red' and 'green') rather than general words (such as 'brightly coloured')
- Do use *concrete* words (such as 'rain' or 'fog) rather than abstract words (such as 'bad weather')
- Do use *plain* words (such as 'began', 'said', 'end') rather than pretentious words (such as 'commenced', 'stated', 'terminated')
- Do not overdress the story with *emotive* or *dramatic* words (such as 'astonishing', 'staggering' or 'sensational). If what you are writing about is any of these things, it will come through without the label
- Do not use *unnecessary* words such as, 'Plans are being drawn up', 'There's more to come later'
- Do not use *unknown quantities* (such as 'very', 'really' and 'quite')
- Do not qualify absolutes. Something is not quite impossible; it is impossible. It is not *glaringly* obvious or *most* essential
- Do not use the word 'incident' when you mean murder, shooting, accident or explosion
- Do not use the word 'just' when it fails to add information as in 'The council leader's just back from London.' Do you mean in the last few seconds, minutes, hours, days or weeks?

In general, think about the language and phrases you use when you write news. You need to pay attention to the detail and think about the effect of the words you use. For example, a man may have *died* after an accident; he probably was not *killed* after one. It would have been very bad luck if he survived the crash but was shot dead two hours later. He was either *killed in* or *died after* the accident. Also, did the man die *following* an accident? Was he really running behind the car when it crashed?

Grammar needs careful attention also. Beware of the singular and plural trap. For example, the council *has*, not the council *have*. However, police are plural and football teams have become that way as well. For example, England *have* won the World Cup, not England *has* won.

There is a school of thought to say some of the basic grammatical rules of writing English are irrelevant on radio. For example, split infinitives which are grammatically incorrect but sound acceptable (the classic *Star Trek* line 'to *boldly* go' instead of 'to go *boldly*'). Each newsroom will have its own style but in general you should try to be grammatically correct without compromising the sound of your news writing.

Writing devices

When you write for the ear, you are simply 'storing' words on paper so that you can tell someone later in the way in which you would speak. Therefore, as we have seen, radio news writing does not always follow the textbook rules of English grammar as you are trying to recreate how you would have spoken. Therefore you need to use a number of writing devices to enable you to make sure that a cue or piece of copy sounds as spontaneous and as natural as possible.

Contractions

You are *telling* the story; therefore what you write should use all the normal contractions used in speech. Contractions make broadcasting sound much more natural and conversational. For example:

It is	becomes	It's
He is	becomes	He's
Do not	becomes	Don't
Should have	becomes	Should've
I am	becomes	I'm

At the start of sentences, it is also better to use a contraction when the third word is 'is'. For example, 'A man's going to make a record attempt . .', or 'A hospital's appealing for more life-saving equipment . . .'.

Punctuation

Use punctuation devices to help you re-create in speech what you have written on paper. Full stops are, of course, essential. Do not use commas or dashes; use dots instead ... like that! It helps the eye of the newsreader pick up the sense of what you are writing far better.

Do not try to read quotations on the radio, especially when they are long. This confuses the listener who may lose track of who is actually saying what. Is it the newsreader or the person he is reporting? Turn quotes into reported speech instead. However, there are certain times when it is acceptable to read quotes on air (see later).

Jargon

Watch out for jargon when writing news stories. The sources of jargon are usually councils or the emergency services. For example, the police and ambulance services use terms like 'fractured femur' when we would say 'broken thigh'.

There is a whole host of other jargon words to watch out for from the police and fire brigades, such as:

Assistance	(help)
Request	(ask)
Terminate	(end)
Decamped	(ran off)
Released	(cut free or sent home)
Sustained injury	(was hurt)
Absconded	(escaped)

Councils are just as bad. Do not let council officers' jargon creep into your news stories. For example, a new building which, according to council papers, is 'detrimental to the visual amenity' is simply 'spoiling the view'.

Fire-fighters often use breathing apparatus. It keeps them alive. There is no need to say it all the time, although it will often appear on voicebank reports from the fire service.

In road accidents (or what the police would call 'road traffic accidents' or 'RTAs'!) try to guard against attributing blame when describing what has happened. For example, 'A man's died after a car crashed into his motorbike on the M25' becomes 'A man's died after a car was in collision with a motorbike on the M25'.

The phrase 'in collision with' is a useful, though clumsy, way of making sure no blame is attributed, even if you are told the circumstances by official sources. Remember though that pedestrians are never 'in collision with' a car. To avoid sounding silly, use the phrase 'involved in an accident with'.

Journalese

A lot of shoddy radio writing is a legacy from newspapers and in particular 'headline English'. This sort of writing was developed by newspaper journalists because it consisted of short words which fitted into the confined space of a headline. These sort of words often do not belong on the radio:

- too often we 'bid' instead of attempt
- we 'slam' instead of criticise
- we 'probe' instead of investigate
- we 'axe' instead of cut
- things are 'massive' instead of big
- more things seem to 'plunge' than fall

Watch out for these words. You can find them most often in the freelance news copy which comes into radio newsrooms written by newspaper people anxious to 'sell' their story by use of hyperbolic language like this. If it is there, rewrite it. It will sound much better.

Clichés

A phrase which has now become a cliché often began life as a useful piece of verbal shorthand. Unfortunately it has become overused to the point where it means nothing. Writing in clichés is a lazy, sloppy way of writing. Make sure you are never guilty of stringing a line of clichés together, even when you are under pressure from a deadline and the temptation is great.

Here are some clichéd words and phrases which detract from the story because they are imprecise, inappropriate or over-used. It is not always possible to avoid using them, but do try and your writing will improve in clarity and precision (Figure 4.1).

Got under way	Blaze	Massive
Got off to a good start	Gutted	Mercy dash
A question mark hangs over	Rushed to hospital	Boss
Grind to a halt	Top secret	Chief
Turn the spotlight on	Grim	Watchdog
In the pipeline	Hit back	Decimate
Up in arms	Potentially lethal	Fulsome praise
At this moment in time	Slammed	Gunned down
The tip of the iceberg	Rapped	Too little, too late
The last straw	Bid	Only time will tell
The ball is in the other court	Probe	Row brewing
Open the floodgates	Brandishing	Last ditch
Tributes pouring in	Wielding	Dawn swoop
Pave the way	Slammed	Dubbed
Trouble flared	Rumpus	Rapped
Limped into port	Grilled	Grim

Figure 4.1 A list of well-worn clichés

Some adjectives come to mind as soon as their noun is mentioned but they are tautological and add little to the sense:

serious danger	all-time record
acute crises	active consideration
mass exodus	high speed chase
brutal murder	fast getaway

Americanisms

There are a lot of techniques we can learn from American radio, but the way Americans have changed the English language is not one of them!

Do watch for the more extreme Americanisms which appear regularly in films and TV drama. Words like 'hospitalised' are familiar on TV but they are not words our listener is likely to use.

Also try to avoid American pronunciation. One of the worst examples is the word 'schedule' which is often heard on air as 'skedule'. If we cannot get our own language correct, it says very little for our credibility!

Names

You should aim for a deliberately informal and conversational style. It should not therefore be necessary to use the prefixes 'Mr' and 'Mrs'.

For example, Tony Blair or John Major is perfectly acceptable. However, prefixes should be used in subsequent references, i.e. Mr Blair or Mr Major. The surname should never be used on its own. This happens in America but in Britain it smacks of disrespect and can be interpreted as bias against the particular individual or party.

Prefixes are not necessary for showbiz or sporting personalities, i.e. John Travolta, Michael Jackson, Ian Botham. The second reference for such people need only be Travolta, Jackson, Botham.

The prefix should also be dropped for criminals such as Peter Sutcliffe, Myra Hindley and Ronnie Biggs, although you must judge whether the use of a prefix later in the story would be unduly respectful.

Use Christian names rather than initials. If you cannot get a Christian name, it sounds better to leave out the name altogether, if possible, rather than using an initial which sounds very odd.

Numbers

Numbers can be tricky to include in stories, especially when they are large. Only use figures if you must. The listener cannot always take in large sums.

Always write the numbers out in your cue or copy so they are easy to read. Mixing words and figures makes it easier to see instantly what the amount is and how to say it:

400,000	becomes	400 thousand
4,600	becomes	4 thousand 6 hundred
£50	becomes	50 pounds
£1.90	becomes	1 pound 90

Never use complex numbers. Always round them up or down:

9.6%	becomes	nearly 10 per cent
£4,898,785	becomes	almost 5 million pounds

To avoid using complicated figures, it often helps to use analogies such as 'the pile of rubbish is now as high as a double-decker bus.'

Avoiding offence

We live in sensitive times. Many of the words and phrases which used to be employed freely are now no longer allowable in normal conversation, never mind news bulletins.

Never use offensive labels. Stick to the facts. If someone is black, then they are black not 'coloured'. Race is not the only thing which can cause problems. Gender is another. It is likely to upset many people if you assume that a certain group is all male (or all female). For example:

> Firemen are at the scene ...
>
> Policemen are warning that ...
>
> The average nurse says she's not paid enough

There are a number of alternatives:

'policemen'	become	'police officers'
'firemen'	become	'fire-fighters'
'ambulance-men'	become	'ambulance crews'
'housewives'	become	'shoppers'
'spokesman'	becomes	'spokeswoman' if applicable (but never 'spokesperson')
'chairman'	becomes	'chairwoman' if applicable (but never 'chair' which is something you sit on!)

However, do not take things to the extreme, where the word is unlikely to be used in everyday speech. You are not a politically-correct mouthpiece. For example, a reporter once referred to a group of tough-looking fishermen as 'fisherfolk'!

Sexual matters can be difficult to describe. Obviously tabloid insults like 'queer' and 'poof' are unacceptable, but 'gay' has become an acceptable synonym for homosexual. If someone is homosexual, do not look for bland euphemisms. They will not thank you and neither will the listener.

Disabled people do not much care for words like 'crippled' either. Someone who has no legs is a 'disabled person' (better than 'handicapped') and has a 'disability'.

One more area where offence can be caused is politics. It is up to politicians to describe their allegiance. If they say they are 'Independent Conservatives' then you must not shorten that to 'Conservative'.

Be careful also of words like 'moderate', 'radical' and 'extremist'. Useful shorthand they may be, but it is not always for us to make these identifications. Extremists, for example, can be a term of abuse. Leave the abuse to politicians – report it by all means, but do not join in, even by accident.

Check the meanings and impact of words you use. The government is technically 'a regime'. But the word is now often used as an insult and is better avoided. If in doubt, look it up. Every newsroom should have a good dictionary. Make it a working tool.

Putting stories in context

It is important that the listener hears the full story in its original context and is not misled by the way it is written. Remember you only get one chance to put over a point on radio. The listener cannot go back and hear what you said, in the way he or she can re-read a newspaper story.

You have a responsibility which is different from a newspaper journalist. You select exactly what stories you want your listener to hear. In newspapers, there are many stories on a page, all with different styles and sizes of headlines to attract attention. On radio, the listener is presented with a single thread of material with no headlines. Importance is determined by position in the bulletin and there are certain rules which make for more logical writing and, as a result, listening.

Attribution

Never start your story with an unattributed statement or controversial claim. It could sound like fact or even the opinion of the radio station. Especially in controversial matters, make sure the listener knows the source of the opinion being expressed at the beginning of the story.

For example, 'Most managers are mean. That's the finding of a new survey out today,' becomes 'A new survey out today claims that most managers are mean.' Each sentence has to be true in itself. For example, it would be wrong to write 'The gap between rich and poor in Britain is growing. That's the claim in a new Labour party report.' Therefore you should write: 'A new Labour party report claims the gap between rich and poor in Britain is growing.'

It also sounds much more natural and gives the listener a better idea of the authority behind the statement. For example, nobody would ever say in normal speech: 'The price of coffee is going up again, according to the grocer.' Instead you would say, 'The grocer says the price of coffee's going up again.' The same principle applies to radio writing, which is trying to achieve this kind of naturalness in speech.

Exaggeration

It becomes very easy sometimes to exaggerate somebody's case. For example, the most dangerous place is on a cue and in-line to a cut: 'Mr Greenslade is denying the claim,' when all in fact he is saying is that there is no evidence to support it. The correct in-line in this case would be: 'Mr Greenslade says there's no proof of the claim.'

You should also aim for much more precision when using words commonly used in tabloid newspaper journalism:

- Has the council 'angrily' rejected a claim against it, or just strongly?
- Is a 'massive police hunt' really underway or is it really a full-scale police search?
- Is the party really 'split' or is it only a small group which is out of step?
- Is that 'row' in the Labour group really 'major' or is the case simply being put by a handful of councillors?

Cause and effect

As already explained, you have just one chance to grab your listener's attention and keep it, so stories must be instantly understandable. So explain the *cause* of what happened before the *effect*.

This is especially important with disasters and death tolls. For example, 'A coach has crashed on the M25 in Essex killing 12 people,' rather than 'Twelve people have been killed and 20 injured on the M25 in Essex when a coach crashed.'

Remember also to think carefully about what the story actually is. Always ask yourself, 'What is the *real* story here?' For example, police may be appealing for witnesses after a woman died in an accident on the M1, but the real story is the *fact* that the woman died in the accident.

Casualty figures

Always pick low estimates of casualty figures, especially in reporting major accidents or disasters. It does no harm to your authority if the death toll rises, but credibility is damaged when dead people come alive!

Organisations

It is not always necessary to give the full name of an organisation, particularly those with long titles. For example, 'train drivers' union' is acceptable for the 'Associated Society of Locomotive Engineers and Firemen' or 'ASLEF'.

Where initials are used, for example, the CBI, the first reference in your story should always be prefaced by a brief description such as 'The employers' organisation, the CBI', or 'The journalists' union, the NUJ.'

Titles

It is more logical in radio for a person's title to come before their name. For example, 'The council chairman Philip Wheeler', rather than the newspaper style of 'Philip Wheeler, council chairman'.

The truth

The single most important part of local radio journalism is to always tell the truth. At the end of every sentence you write, ask yourself whether what you have just written is strictly accurate. There are frequently untruths in news writing. For example, the use of plural for singular as in 'Tory councillors are demanding . . .' when you know of only one councillor.

5

News bulletins

The news agenda

The news bulletin is the showcase of the radio journalist. It is the chance to give the listener a good idea of what is happening in just a few minutes.

Bulletins are governed by a radio station's news agenda: the policy set which determines which stories are covered in what way and in what style.

Your target listener

All newsrooms, commercial and BBC, have different news agendas and it is impossible to generalise. However, the starting point for the news agenda is likely to be the radio station's target audience, determined by the Programme Director or Managing Editor. The news bulletins therefore focus on the stories that interest their listener. The listener is interested in news primarily when it affects him or her personally. This could be through the pocket (a tax increase) or through the emotions (a badly treated child).

Other such stories could include, for example:

- the environment (not just the 'green' thing, but what is happening around)
- the economy (mortgages, wages, the cost of living)
- crime (how safe is it on the streets? What is being done?)
- health (doctors, hospitals, the NHS)
- education (the state of schools, teaching methods)
- transport and travel (roads and railways)

- sport and leisure (big teams and major pastimes)
- national politics (the personalities and their policies)
- local politics (what is happening of countywide or national significance)

Some commercial stations, especially those in the GWR group, have conducted detailed research into what sort of stories their target listeners want to hear. As a result, they have adjusted their news agenda to highlight environmental and health stories. In addition, to ensure their audience know when these stories are about to be included, they are 'signposted' or 'flagged' within news bulletins with a tag saying 'Health news . . .' or 'Environment news . . .'.

Other stations are moving away from traditional news values and concentrating almost entirely on 'news you can use' such as consumer stories and health issues. When they do stories about accidents, for example, they focus not on the accident itself but more on the disruption caused.

The majority of UK stations, though, continue to be influenced by the traditional news values of the BBC with many programmers regarding the local news bulletins as a way of injecting real-life, relatable, local drama into their music output.

Whatever a station's news values, it is all about competing for the listener's attention. The day has long gone when 'listening to the news' was a solemn rite, marked by the family dropping all other activities to gather round the radio set.

It is not that people are less interested in the news. What has happened is that the whole pattern of living has changes,. The family circle is now less close, there are frequent interruptions as well as other activities and interests.

Now all radio stations must compete for attention. Radio can no longer 'command' an audience. Radio must *woo* it. That is the challenge.

It is not enough merely to broadcast news. It is your job to make sure that news is listened to *and understood*. To inform, we must interest.

Relevance

The key consideration in whether or not to include an item in a news bulletin is its *relevance*. Each story must earn its place in the bulletin by having an effect on the listener's life as determined by the target focus of the news agenda. This effect can be directly through say, the listener's council tax being increased, or indirectly by something which triggers the listener's emotions through sympathy or empathy.

When making editorial judgements, you should always ask yourself: What does this *mean* to my listener?

Be careful with world news on local radio. Some stations, especially BBC ones, have a policy of including a high proportion of international news. But others, including many commercial stations, prefer to concentrate on home news. A well-known test at a radio training centre used to give students a news story about rebels blockading a port in Ceylon. What was the relevance of the story to the listener in Britain? Many thought it had little – until they found out it would affect supplies of tea!

Also watch stories which come from council chambers. Many of them are very dull tales of petty political infighting or things which people generally neither care about nor understand. Unless there is a story which really does affect someone outside the councils (such as dustbins being collected, roads being built, or schools being shut), think twice about covering it. As a general rule, go with stories which affect *people*. Ditch those which do not.

It is all about balance and judgement. A radio journalist running a busy newsdesk has to weigh the important against the interesting many times a day.

Quality versus quantity

If a news item needs artificial support to help it stand up, it is not really worth telling. It is an unfortunate fact that many local radio stations throw at their listener a barrage of dull and boring stories simply because they are trying to fill a mythical 'quota' of local news. Quality should never suffer for the sake of quantity. The listener soon notices.

Place names

You are working in local radio. Local stories must be just that. Try to emphasise the local angle in all your stories. For example, 'Police are warning women not to walk alone at night after a series of attacks. The call comes after three indecent assaults in Chelmsford . . .' becomes 'Police in Chelmsford are warning women not to walk alone at night after three indecent assaults . . .'.

Also try to get as many place names in your bulletins as possible by frequently including lots of short, two-line copy stories from around your area. It quickens the pace of a bulletin and makes your listener feel as though you are covering his or her town or village even though you do not always have reporters on the ground. If you find an excuse for giving a list of place names then do it, within reason.

The 'life' of a story

Stories need freshening as much as possible. If you are working on a story for the following morning's breakfast bulletins, try to provide an alternative cut or clip with a different angle in the cue. This helps provide variety in the bulletin. Generally, a story will last for no more than three consecutive broadcasts. After that, it should be dropped or rewritten completely. With constantly changing and fast-moving stories, it is easy to freshen each hour and the benefits of doing this – whatever the pressures in the newsroom – are enormous; the listener feels up to date from hour to hour.

Bulletin essentials

Accuracy

There is no excuse for sloppy, inaccurate reporting. You must check all the facts and make sure they are correct. If the story comes from the police, make sure you have spoken to the right person – a duty inspector, station sergeant or press officer. If you are making factual statements, make sure you know your facts or check them.

The best advice is *check, check and check again*. If accuracy falls down, so does the radio station's credibility – and with it your own journalistic reputation.

There is an old journalistic maxim which is still relevant today as it was years ago: 'When in doubt, find out. If still in doubt, leave out.'

Taste

Be careful not to upset your listener unnecessarily with tasteless gory detail. Some things are gruesome and horrible enough. Remember that your listener may be eating, drinking or playing with the children while listening to the radio. Torsos being cut up or blood-

and-guts stories just do not go down well with a family at the breakfast table.

Never run a story simply to excite your listener with sex or violence. Naturally, when there are grounds for public concern, stories involving sex and violence have to be covered; for example, a child cruelty case which the social services department should have prevented. However, try to emphasise the reason for legitimate public concern.

When describing a rape, it is sufficient to say 'raped' rather than 'brutally' or 'violently' raped.

When you have to describe acts of violence, you should avoid excitable language. Remember understatement is often more effective and has more impact. For example, 'The man was blasted in the head with a sawn-off shotgun and left lying in a pool of blood,' becomes 'A man came up behind him and shot him once in the head.'

Balance and fairness

It is the job of a radio newsroom to reflect all opinions and give people criticised on the air the opportunity to reply. A balance may not necessarily be achieved within one bulletin, but over a period of time. For example, if a protester criticises the chairman of the education committee about a school's closure on the 8am news bulletin on Monday morning, it would be appropriate to have the education committee chairman's reply to that on the 8am news bulletin on Tuesday morning. This allows both sides of the argument to reach the same audience, albeit on consecutive days.

Tone

As well as being clear and concise, a good radio news bulletin should be authoritative and non-patronising, never insulting the intelligence of your listener. All you need to do is remember these guiding principles and they should automatically be reflected in the tone of your writing.

Comment

Needless to say, you should avoid commenting at all on any story. Your job is to be dispassionate and objective. Remember that your view on a story can sometimes be detected by the tone in which you read it on air. Beware and play it straight.

Cues – a working example

The cue into audio is the link between the reporter, the bulletin presenter and the listener. Ideally, the listener will understand exactly what the reporter is saying through the medium of the presenter. However, this ideal may stand or fall on the quality of the cue. Let us look at a working example of how a cue develops and some of the pitfalls in cue writing (Figure 5.1).

Chantler	22.10.96	pm bulls

EMBARGOED UNTIL 1300

HOSPITAL/Franklin

    More than 200 beds are set to close at St John's Hospital because of government spending restrictions.
    The warning has come from the district health authority . . . which needs to save 1million by the end of next year.
    But the decision is angering some city councillors . . . who say the health authority is already struggling through lack of cash brought about by previous government rulings.
    Labour's Mark Franklin . . . who represents Witham ward . . . says the government is trying to run down the health service at the expense of people in the area . . .

CART:	Hospital/Franklin	
DUR:	24"	
OUT:	. . . harder all the time.	(54")

Figure 5.1 A typical cue

The topline

A good cue has the story 'up top' but, as we saw earlier, not all in the first line. Cramming too much into the topline confuses the listener:

> More than 2 hundred beds are set to close at St John's Hospital in the coming year because the district health authority has been forced to save one million pounds to meet government spending targets.

That is the essence of the story, but you probably had to read it twice to get the sense of it and anyone hearing the words read aloud would certainly lose track somewhere. A better way of writing the cue and topline would be:

> More than 2 hundred beds are set to close at St John's
> Hospital because of government spending restrictions.
>
> The warning has come from the health authority . . .
> which needs to save one million pounds by the end of
> next year.

By dividing the story into two shorter sentences it becomes much
easier to understand first time round – and remember the listener has
only one chance to hear it. By contrast, a newspaper story can be read
again and again.

Going into detail

Having started the story with your topline, you need to expand on it.
However, be careful of making the cue too long as the listener may
become bored with the story before the audio is played. A good cue
provides the context for the audio which follows; it is not intended to
tell the whole story unaided.

However, you may add something like:

> But the decision is angering some city councillors . . . who
> say the health authority is already struggling through lack
> of cash brought about by previous government rulings.

This paragraph prepares our listener to hear an angry councillor. But
try not to be led astray into exhaustive detail of previous spending cuts,
a list of 12 other hospitals in the county affected by economies, or what
the BMA said about the government last June. In a long newspaper
article, they would all have their place, but you have perhaps one minute
or less to tell the whole story – including the audio cut.

Into the audio

A good middle paragraph in a cue sets the stage for the audio cut which
follows. We go into the actual audio with an 'in-line' like this:

> Labour's Mark Franklin .. who represents Witham ward . . .
> says the government is trying to run down the health service
> at the expense of people in the area.

The audio cut

The words of Mr Franklin which follow should add something fresh. Avoid, at all costs, a 'double cue'. The above example would be a 'double cue' if his first words were: 'This government is trying to run down the NHS at the expense of people in the area.'

If those were his first words, we need a complementary in-line like:

> Labour's Mark Franklin . . . who represents Witham ward
> . . . says these new economies will hit everyone . . .

A double cue should be avoided because it tells the listener exactly what he or she is about to hear, so taking all the dramatic impact out of the audio which follows and making it superfluous. Radio news is all about *impact*.

Cue layout

Every radio station has its own style of cue layout, but any cue should include the following essentials:

- the date
- the reporter's name or initials
- a name for the story (known as the 'catchline' or 'slug')
- the cue itself
- the duration of the audio cut
- the out-cue of the audio cut
- the total running time of the cue (calculated by reading the cue to yourself or by counting three words to a second)
- any special notes to help the bulletin editor

Cues should be arranged simply and logically. Avoid using capital letters throughout except for strong emphasis and for complicated names and places.

Start a new paragraph for each sentence and indent it at the beginning of the line; this helps the cue's 'readability' as the eye finds it easier to pick up indents. It also helps to see how long you have to go before taking a breath when reading!

Keep to the same catchlines or slugs for each story and updates to avoid confusion between stories. Add the letters 'rw' for rewrites, 'ud' for updates and 'add' for additional copy.

6

News presentation

Reading the news

A good news presenter or newsreader can make even dull stories sound reasonably interesting but a poor presenter can kill a hot story by reading it incompetently. What is the point in everyone putting in all the hard work if the presentation is sub-standard?

Sound interested

A ground rule for news presentation is that you must be actually *interested* in the material. That means sound interested. If you do not care – and let it show – the listener is very unlikely to bother either.

Understand the story

You must understand every story in your bulletin. You depend heavily on the reporters who wrote the copy but, because you must understand news to present it, never hesitate to query something which is uncertain. If you have to ask about it, the chances are high that the listener, who cannot ask questions of anyone, will be left completely in the dark.

Check

Do not, unless there is no alternative, read copy on the air unseen. It is too easy to misread something and realise only as the words are leaving your mouth that you have placed completely the wrong emphasis on the story. Read all your copy out loud in advance if you can. A few minutes spent on rehearsal is never wasted.

Technically speaking

A well-read bulletin can be spoilt by a silly technical mistake. For example, 'I'm sorry about that, we'll try to bring you that report in our next bulletin', or 'I'm sorry, that wasn't the Prime Minister . . . it was the secretary of the Farmers' Union.'

These embarrassing and unprofessional slips can usually be avoided. If you 'drive' the bulletin yourself, check your carts or touchscreen menu. Is the audio all cued properly? Is it all in the right order? Have you got all the audio you need at your fingertips? If someone else drives the bulletin, have they got all the audio? Do they understand the order in which the audio must be played? Do they know which story might be dropped if there is an overrun? It may be praiseworthy to 'get out' of a technical error with aplomb, but a thousand times better not to let it happen in the first place.

Breathe in . . .

There are a number of good books on voice production and if you have any doubts about your own abilities, read one of them. Be aware, though, that such books are frequently intended for actors, not broadcasters. There is not the same requirement to 'project' your voice on radio because the microphone will amplify it for you. So do not shout. But do sit up straight and breathe properly. This means a couple of deep inhalations before you start. If you try to speak on almost empty lungs, your voice will sound thin and strained and you will feel uncomfortable.

During the bulletin, remember to keep breathing! That sounds odd, perhaps, but the right place to breathe is at the end of a sentence, not halfway through it. Use audio as a chance to take a couple more deep breaths if you feel nervous. Deep breathing – within reason – has a curiously calming effect.

Keep level

Strange rises and falls in your tone of voice will puzzle and maybe amuse the listener. Do not strain to speak much lower or higher than is comfortable for you. Also, steer midway between a monotone and 'singing' the bulletin.

Pronunciation

The BBC publishes an excellent pronunciation dictionary which is well worth having in the newsroom (you do not have to be a BBC station!). Unless you are sure, ask other people about unusual words – another good reason for checking your copy first. Listen, too, when other radio and TV news bulletins are broadcast. The chances are high that network television and radio will get the pronunciation correct because they have so many more resources on which to call if they need to check unusual words.

Foreign names are the worst. As the last resort, if you are not sure, take a deep breath, say the word confidently as well as you can and carry on. If it really is unusual, the listener probably knows no better. But take the first chance you get to check it. Local place names on local radio stations must be pronounced correctly. Make sure your station has a phonetic list of the difficult or tricky names (Figure 6.1).

Tone

It is vital to get the tone of your news presentation just right. You need to sound authoritative yet natural and informal. Each story has its own 'atmosphere'. You need to pitch the speed of your reading just right and inject the correct amount of 'light' and 'shade' in your voice. Talking fast and loud does not mean you sound more urgent or dramatic; often it is quite the reverse. As in many things, the key is in finding the correct balance. Practice as often as you can – and seek the opinion of others. Get a feel for your voice; how high it can go, how long it can go. Find a natural level for your voice.

Listen

It is very difficult to know how you sound without listening to a recording. So make an 'aircheck' of your bulletins regularly. Record a bulletin every week or two and listen to it afterwards. It is not ego-tripping; it is sensible and professional monitoring of your performance.

NEWS PRONUNCIATIONS

Parvez LATIF	UK	paarváyz lătéef
Zvid GAMSAKHURDIA	USSR (former)	zvee-ádd gamssăchóordi-ă
SUKHUMI		soochóomi (-*ch* as in Sc. 'loch')
ZUGDIDI		zoog-dyéedi
Ruslan KHASBULATOV		rŏossláan *ch*assbŏolátŏf (-*ch* as in Sc. 'loch')
DUSCHANBE		dooshanbáy
Yevgeniy SHAPOSHNIKOV		yĕvgáyni sháapŏshnikŏf
Andrey KOZYREV		andráy kózzirĕf
CHADLI Bin Jadeed	Algeria	shádli bin jădéed (-j as in 'Jack')
Abasi MADANI		ăbáassi máddăni
Ali BELHAJJ		álee bell-hájj (-j as in 'Jack')
Mohammed BOUDIAF		mŏ-hámmĕd bood-yáaf
Hocine AIT-AHMED		hŏossáyn īt áachmĕd (-ī as in 'high')
Abdul Hamid MEHRI		ábdŏol hăméed mé-hri (-me as in 'met')
TEHIYA	Israel	te-hee-yáa
MOLEDET		moléddet
Yuval NE'EMAN		yoovál nay-ĕmáan
Rehavam ZE'EVI		rĕchăvám zĕ-ayvée
Anand PANYARACHUN	Thailand	annúnn pún-yarrătchóon (-u as in 'but')
VO VAN KIET	Vietnam	vó vún kyétt (-u as in 'but')

Figure 6.1 The BBC daily pronunciation list. *Courtesy: BBC*

Figure 6.2 The bulletin desk at BBC GLR. Note the GNS logger tape machine and the cart stack to its left. The Duty Producer can use the loudspeaker to monitor station output or the material from GNS as it is fed. *Courtesy: Sarah Cavan*

Microphones

The microphone is a sensitive piece of equipment which will amplify everything it can. That means your voice, your breathing, the rustle of clothing, the squeak of a chair, the rustle of scripts and the clunk of a cart. So when a microphone is open, move and act with care.

Distance from the microphone is important. Too close and the smack of lips and pop of consonants will make the bulletin unpleasant to hear. Too far away and you will be curiously distant, with extra reverberation making listening difficult. Also, if you are too far away, the increase in gain which will be necessary to compensate can make the microphone even more sensitive to unwanted noise.

Stress

You can tell the listener which words are important in a story by stressing them. You are the interpreter of news for the listener and if you do not stress the appropriate words, the listener will not get the idea. You may also lose the listener's attention entirely.

For example, here is a news voicer:

> The Prime Minister arrived at 10 Downing Street early this morning to start his first day at work. He went in by the front door just after eight o'clock, refusing to respond to reporters, although he did give them a wave and a smile. One of his first tasks will be the formation of a new Cabinet. Last night, there was mounting speculation that he is considering a major reshuffle and, during this morning, the arrivals of various party figures at Downing Street have been closely watched. Sources close to the Prime Minister say he is considering new people for the jobs of Chancellor and Foreign Secretary and of course he will have to find a new Transport Secretary. But so far, no names have been announced. This is Sarah Revell at Downing Street.

What words would you stress? Underline those that you think are important with a pencil and then compare them to the version below.

Here is the same voicer, with good stress words emphasised. Do not worry if you did not get them all. Try reading the piece out loud, with your stresses, and then read it again with these:

> The *Prime Minister* arrived at 10 Downing Street *early* this morning to start his *first* day at work. He went in by the front door just after eight o'clock, *refusing* to respond to reporters, although he *did* give them a wave and a smile. One of his *first* tasks will be the formation of a new *Cabinet*. Last night, there was *mounting* speculation that he is considering a *major* reshuffle and, during this morning, the *arrivals* of various party figures at Downing Street have been *closely* watched. Sources close to the Prime Minister say he is considering *new* people for the jobs of *Chancellor* and *Foreign* Secretary and of course he will have to find a new Transport Secretary. But *so far*, *no* names have been announced. This is Sarah Revell at Downing Street.

Notice that the stresses are very particular: *Foreign* needs a stress (it is probably the first time that this particular job has been mentioned in the reshuffle), but *Secretary* is a word used for a number of Cabinet posts and does not need such emphasis. Also, there is an implication that everyone already knows that a new Transport Secretary will be needed – so no stress on that phrase.

Making a stress is not simply a matter of speaking more loudly; try pausing slightly before a stress word – let it sink in for the listener.

Quotations

Quotations need a special kind of stress. For example, in the sentence: 'The Prime Minister accused the Opposition of "cowardice and hypocrisy" over the issue . . .', a pause on each side of the quotation helps to make it clearer that these were the Prime Minister's actual words.

Corrections

Sometimes, you simply get something wrong. It might be your fault because you mis-read the copy, or someone else's because their mistake was not seen in time. If you know as you say it that something is wrong, an immediate correction is best: '. . . that should be *forty-two* thousand . . .'; or 'I'm sorry, that should be *Watford* football club.'

Try not to make too much of a big deal of any correction like this. Simply say it and carry on with the same tone of voice as before. If you sound worried or thrown off your stride, the listener is likely to take it more seriously too.

Going back to a story later in the bulletin because it was wrong the first time is more noticeable. This is an editorial decision, but if you have made a mistake and it could be serious, as in a court case, there is probably no alternative than to refer back to the story and broadcast the correction. *Do not* repeat the original mistake if you can help it – simply put the correction in context and keep it as simple as possible. For example, 'As you may have heard earlier in the bulletin, a man from Tolworth Cross was jailed for rape at the city's Crown Court today. We'd like to make it clear that his name was *John* Smith.'

Self-op bulletins

Traditionally, news on radio was read by one person with someone else performing the technical functions. This is still the case in some network stations, where a team can be involved in getting the bulletin to air. Some local stations still have someone other than the news presenter playing in the audio, opening the microphone and so on, but this person is often the programme presenter who is on duty anyway (Figure 6.2).

Figure 6.3 Journalist Elouise Twisk presenting a self-op news bulletin at BBC Essex

Increasingly the presenter at a local station presses a button or opens a fader marked 'News' at the appropriate moment and the bulletin presenter takes over entirely. These bulletins are known as 'self-op' (self-operated) bulletins (Figure 6.3).

Getting ready

If you are wise, you will be in the studio several minutes early. That is not because the bulletin might start early (it certainly should not!), but so that you can prepare and be ready to go. The best bulletins are not read, never mind driven, by a breathless presenter who has just been pounding up a flight of stairs to the news studio with only seconds to spare. In some newsrooms, there is a bravado about rushing into the studio at the last moment. It seems some journalists think this makes the news more up to date. Have none of it; the listener will only notice an ill-prepared and poorly presented bulletin. To combat this, some newsrooms have a five-minute 'gate' before a bulletin where the presenter has to be in the studio to prepare and nothing extra except the most urgent of updates can be added to the bulletin as prepared.

In the studio

Once in the studio, check the audio (either the carts or the on-screen computer menu) and check the cues and copy. Do you have something missing? Another reason for arriving early is that any discrepancy found at this stage can be put right, if there is talkback to the newsroom. With luck, someone else can bring you the missing cart or cue in time.

In analogue newsrooms, insert the carts into the stack and, if the equipment allows, fast re-cue them. However, be careful that you do not let this re-cueing process go on dangerously near to the start of the bulletin. (You will feel foolish if your lead cart is still re-cueing when it is needed). All carts should be cued anyway, but this is a good piece of extra insurance. In computerised newsrooms, touch the screen or activate the mouse on each audio cut to check it is cued properly.

Check that the cues and the audio are in the same order and that your mixing desk is monitoring the correct output. If you are not getting the right programme cue off air, you will not know when to start your bulletin and you may not be able to hear your own audio when you play it. In these days of multifrequency networked local stations with split programming, getting the wrong programme cue is a real possibility. Once again, check in good time.

Adjust your headphones to the most comfortable volume setting. Remember that some mixing desks monitor 'processed' off air. This means the off-air signal you hear will have gone through an audio processor or compressor to boost the high and low frequencies and make the output more punchy. If you are not used to this, it can be off-putting. Some presenters read the bulletin with one headphone on and one off in order to hear the 'natural' sound of their voice while also hearing the audio cuts and the processed sound. Do whatever it is that makes you feel most comfortable.

Here is the news . . .

Take a couple of deep breaths, then open your microphone while the news jingle – if there is one – is playing, not when it has stopped or faded out completely. Start confidently, with one finger above the cart's 'fire' button for the first piece of audio or ready to touch the computer playout screen.

In analogue studios, as each piece of audio plays, 'update' the stack by removing the played carts and replacing them. Always have the next two carts ready to play. Should the first fail, the rattle of a hastily-inserted cart always sounds dreadful in a bulletin – so have another one ready to go.

If you are reading a bulletin which has a 'clock' finish (it ends at a precise time, to the second), keep the top two copy stories on one side where you can easily find them again, for reasons we will discuss shortly.

When things go wrong . . .

If something fails in spite of all your precautions, keep calm. This is your bulletin and the listener will take a cue from you. If you seem rattled or nervous, the listener will think something really serious has gone wrong. But do have some insurance. Have some extra copy stories with you that do not have to be used. Then, if you lose some audio, you have some additional material. It is not impossible for a complete cart stack to fail or a computer system 'crash' to occur during a live bulletin. With the extra copy, you should be able to keep going.

This is why we suggested keeping the top two stories on one side. If you have to end precisely on time, or if a failure has left you ridiculously short, you can always refer back to them for the last 30 seconds or so of the bulletin: ' ... and finally, the main stories again this hour . . .'. This may seem a gesture of desperation, but it actually sounds rather slick and urgent. The listener simply will not realise you are filling for time, especially if you sound confident. Some stations, incidentally, repeat the main story at the end of the bulletin as a matter of policy.

Only if all else fails should you end a bulletin early and then only if you are sure the succeeding programme is ready to take over. Nothing sounds worse than a silence after the bulletin. You are also unfairly giving the listener the impression that it is the next presenter who is in the wrong by not being ready.

If there is a failure, and it must be explained, do so in terms the listener will understand. *Never* say: 'I'm sorry that cart wasn't cued,' but rather: 'I'm sorry we can't bring you that report . . .' The listener understandably thinks a cart is something pulled by a horse!

Remember that mistakes which are obvious enough to you may not be so apparent to the listener. If you read a cue and the audio fails to fire, think before leaping in with an apology. A good audio cue will stand alone, if necessary. Do not apologise for something unless the failure is evident. If you can simply carry on, do so.

7

Technicalities

Audio recording

All radio stations rely on different types of recording systems to store interviews and audio and play out programme material. Older stations use analogue equipment such as cartridge players and open-reel tape recorders. Becoming more common, though, is digital equipment where audio is recorded direct onto a computer hard disk which can then be edited, stored, played out and archived.

Analogue recording

Analogue recordings use tape to reproduce sound. For many years, analogue recording was the traditional way of storing and playing out sound in radio stations. It is important to know a little of how sound is actually recorded to help understand the editing process.

A device sensitive to variations in air pressure caused by sound waves – a microphone – is used to produce a small fluctuating electrical signal. This signal is boosted and passed to a recording head on the tape recorder, which generates a distinctive magnetic field. The particles of oxide on the passing tape are disturbed by this field and assume a new pattern in response. This pattern of oxide particles remains 'frozen' on the tape, until disturbed by another magnetic field.

If the tape is run past a playback head, the pattern of particles is 'read' by the head, which produces another signal in turn. This signal, duly amplified, is sent to a loudspeaker – broadly a microphone in reverse – so producing audible sound once again.

Although the current generated in a playback head is very similar to

Figure 7.1 The Uher has been the standard open-reel portable machine for many years. It is rugged and well-built, but is now being replaced by smaller cassette machines

the original, various changes can occur during the process which are all technically known as 'distortion'. One major distortion of the reproduced signal is caused by background noise on the tape which cannot be entirely eliminated, although it has been reduced remarkably by ingenious circuits in modern analogue recorders.

Analogue equipment includes the following:

Open-reel tape recorders use spools of varying sizes containing ¼-inch tape playing at speeds ranging from 3¾ to 15 inches per second (i.p.s) . Open reel machines made by companies such as Revox and Studer are found in studios; the most common portable machine is still the Uher (Figures 7.1 and 7.2).

Figure 7.2 The base model Revox tape recorder – a B77 with dust cover. Virtually the standard machine for newsrooms

Figure 7.3 Marantz are one of the main suppliers of broadcast-quality cassette recorders. This is a lightweight and reliable machine

Cassette recorders use reel-to-reel tape enclosed in a plastic box. The tape is much narrower than open reel at $1/8$th inch and running at a slower speed of $1^7/8$ inches enabling total running times from ten to 120 minutes. Originally, cassettes were intended for home use only but have improved in quality so much that machines such as the Marantz (Figure 7.3) or Sony Professional Walkman are now the most commonly used form of portable broadcast recording. Because cassettes contain narrow tape which is difficult to edit, recordings are usually transferred to open-reel machines for editing. However, with luck, sometimes it is possible to put a clip directly from cassette onto cartridge for broadcast. Usually, though, editing will be required for a 'clean' sound without any 'zips' or 'wows' at the beginning.

Cartridge machines use cartridges or 'carts' which contain a continuous loop of quarter-inch tape enclosed in a plastic case, rather like a square, oversize cassette. The running time can be anything from 10 seconds to 10 minutes. When a cart is recorded, an inaudible tone is placed on the tape at the start point. The tape then runs until the same tone is detected which causes it to stop, ready to play again at the touch of the play button (Figure 7.4). Carts, therefore, are self-cueing devices. Usually, cart machines do not contain any kind of erase head. Carts are cleaned with a bulk erasing device, which generates a strong magnetic field. A cart used for recording without being cleaned or 'bulked' will retain the original recording underneath the new one and both will be heard. Such a cart is said to be 'dirty'. Some cart machines have a special erase mode, but this must be used before recording. The two functions cannot be used together.

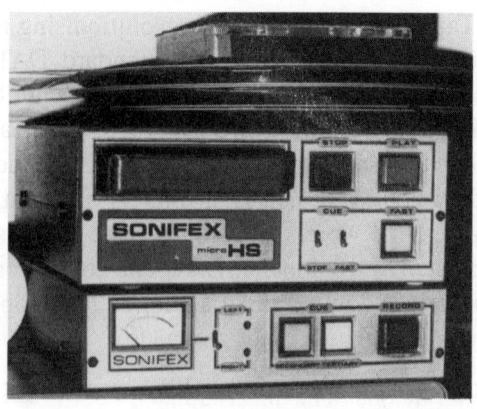

Figure 7.4 A cart machine made by Sonifex, with recording module underneath

Tape machines for news operations in radio stations use a standard speed of 7½ i.p.s. Slower speeds are not much used because quality suffers. Higher speeds are mainly used for music as this makes for easier editing because the sounds are more 'spread out'. Although speeds should be left set on 7½ i.p.s. on news machines, accidents can happen – so check, especially before playing a tape directly to air.

Recorders are generally full tape width stereo machines, adjusted for news purposes to use one track only. The other track is still recorded, but only with silence. This means you cannot turn the tape over and use it in the other direction.

Digital recording

Digitised audio signals have now been with us for some time and the basic technique is in daily domestic use with compact discs.

With powerful computers also becoming commonplace in the form of personal computers (PCs) and with vast amounts of digital storage also becoming cheaper, a revolution is taking place in the way radio stations operate. Steadily improving software for the compression and decompression of digital signals representing speech and stereo music means that recording, editing, storage and transmission can now be much more efficient.

Digital recording hardware and software includes:

Digital Audio Tape or DAT for short is revolutionising recording and editing and is now regarded as the industry standard. DATs are smaller in size than analogue cassettes and use the same technology as video recorders – a slow speed tape scanned by a revolving head. The signal is recorded in digital form in which the original electrical variations are represented by a series of pulses or 'bits' of information. Audio in 'bit' form is rather like words typed on a word processor; both can easily be manipulated by a computer. The sound quality remains exactly the same as the original and, unlike analogue tape copies, does not degrade as successive digital copies are made.

Digital cartridges do not use tape at all but record digitally and play back a floppy disk. Usually, a digital cart carries various items such as clips, jingles or commercials. Unlike the tape cart, it does not need to be rewound so that any of its tracks is instantly accessible. Its other major advantage over tape carts is that digital carts never become tangled and rarely jam.

Minidiscs are smaller, recordable compact discs usually capable of holding more than 70 minutes of fully indexible, instantly accessible sound. They are used mainly for jingles and backing music but can be used for audio clips and commercials. Both minidiscs and digital cartridges have their own digital players, usually with a large rotary control on the front to select the desired track. A digital display shows the title of the track selected and its number. These do, however, use digital compression, so the quality will degrade with successive copies.

Computer hard disk is a studio-based system with a fully interactive massive memory capacity used by many modern radio stations to store all audio from music to jingles, commercials to news clips. Once audio is loaded onto the system as data, any number of individual users can access it simultaneously and independently stop it, start it, edit it or put it on pause, all without any denigration in quality. Because it is computer data, it is also immediately accessible. Hard disk is the best way to make quality material instantly available to a number of users.

Portable hard disk is the new generation of location recorder. These are small, rugged and robust portable recorders, such as the Courier machine made by Sonifex, where audio is captured on hard disk. It can be digitally edited on location using a 'graphical scrub wheel' and played back via ISDN or mobile phone. Prices for these machines will eventually become more affordable and it is likely they will become standard reporter's equipment for digital newsrooms in the next few years.

Audio editing

Audio often has to be edited before transmission to remove unwanted parts of a recording. In an interview, people tend to cough, pause, make false starts and other mistakes; all these events are annoying for the listener and, if left untouched, would waste valuable time in a news bulletin.

Editing should never be used to change the sense of what someone is saying. It is not acceptable, for example, to splice together a question and answer which did not actually occur together in the original conversation.

Remember to take out any reference to material already edited out. You will confuse the listener if you leave in things like 'As I said before . . .', and 'I tell you again . . .'.

You should interview in such a way that editing is reduced to a minimum. It takes a lot of time and tends to be more difficult to do just before the audio is wanted. The tension of an approaching deadline makes a lot of us less nimble-fingered.

Be careful when editing. Done properly, your expertise should not be noticed by the listener because a good edit goes unheard. That is one reason why recordings have been treated with caution for many years as potential legal evidence – they are too easy to change.

Fluffs and unnecessary hesitations can be remedied. However, remember that 'cleaning up' an interview has its dangers. A pause before an interviewee replies to a penetrating question may be editorially significant and should be kept. Only if it is a loss of concentration is it right to remove it.

Taking care means listening to how your interviewee speaks and making sure you preserve the natural rhythm of that speech by meticulously observing breath pauses. Two breaths cut together sound ridiculous, but it is easily done. If, on the other hand, you remove all breath pauses in a sentence, the statements sound as if they have come from a robot. So, with tape editing, the golden rule is to listen twice – cut once, as you could destroy the original. An advantage of modern digital equipment means you can cut and copy as often as you like without destroying the original.

Figure 7.5 Journalist David Whiteley editing tape on a Revox machine at Essex FM

Analogue editing

Apart from your tape, a machine and headphones, you will need the following tools for analogue open-reel tape editing:

- splicing tape
- a Chinograph pencil
- a razor blade
- a splicing block

Splicing tape is specially made for the job. It is not too sticky and just narrower than the recording tape. Any other sticky tape cannot be used as a substitute. It may not stick properly, be too thick, or allow adhesive to leak onto the vulnerable heads of tape machines (Figure 7.5).

We will assume you need to edit five seconds of silence out of an interview. Place your machine in the editing mode. This varies from model to model, but the aim is to hear the tape as you make it back and forth in front of the playback head.

Note that most professional machines have three heads. From left to right in the tape channel (the direction of tape travel) the heads are erase, record and playback. You must edit on the playback head, at the right of the channel.

Find the end of the audio you wish to keep and move the tape until you are just past it, by perhaps a quarter of a centimetre. Mark this spot using your Chinograph pencil, making a short vertical line. Do not let your line stray off the sides of the tape – the pencil will mark the head itself just as easily and reduce the sound quality until it can be cleaned off again.

Now move the tape to the right, until you hear the next word which you wish to keep. Put a second mark just to the right of the word.

Remove the tape from the channel and put it along the splicing block. Using the 45-degree cut, cut the tape at each Chinograph mark. Put the centre section (the short piece) on one side – do not lose it yet. Butt the free ends of the remaining tape together in the splicing block but do not overlap them (it is easily done!).

Place a piece of splicing tape about three centimetres long over the join, parallel with the tape and not overlapping it on either side. It is easiest to cut a length of splicing tape in advance and pick it up with the edge of your blade. Do not touch the splicing tape with your fingers more than necessary, as the oils in your skin will make it stick less well. Place over the join and press it down with your fingers. Then gently remove the tape from the block. The splicing tape should cover each side of the join equally. A good splice is as strong as the original tape. Finally, play back the spliced portion at normal speed. If all is well, you can now discard the short section you cut out.

If you want to add a pause, some wildtrack from the original interview is the proper solution, but if it must be silence, use blank tape and never coloured leader tape. This will not record and will ruin any future recordings made on the same tape.

Digital editing

The most common sort of digital editing is on-screen on a computer. The audio is transferred onto the hard disk of a newsroom or radio station computer system. Using suitable software, you can view the data as a waveform. By using a mouse to point to and highlight the relevant sections of audio, you can cut and re-order the material. This method can also create fades and other effects, while leaving the original recording intact. This means it is easy to experiment with possible edits until you obtain the desired result (Figure 7.6).

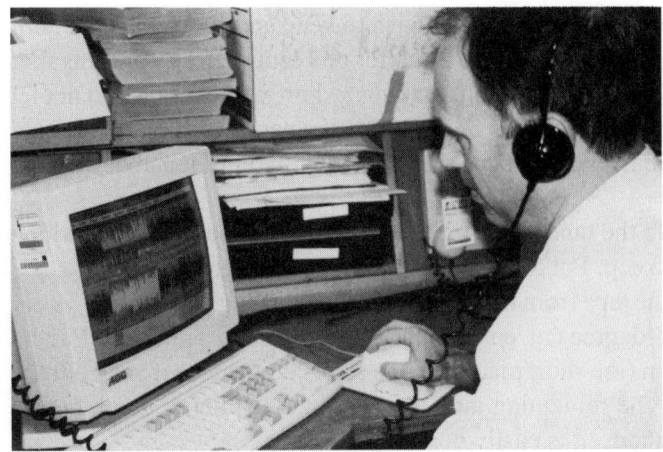

Figure 7.6 Senior BBC Essex journalist Charlie Partridge editing by computer. Note how the sound appears on screen as a waveform

The other method of digital editing involves an expensive digital editing suite which uses at least two DAT machines and an edit controller. The controller uses time-code information on the original recording as a 'label' for each part of the audio. You can then re-assemble these parts in whatever order you need.

Computerised newsrooms

The paper-free and tape-free environment

The development of computerised newsrooms has moved quickly over the past few years. Getting information quickly and processing it fast are what news is all about. Computerised newsrooms therefore make life easier and more efficient for journalists, cutting down on paper, making information available to more users and allowing almost instant recall of items from powerful databases. Equipment to create a paper-less and tape-less environment is becoming much more economical and accessible (Figures 7.7a and b).

Many high-tech companies have been good at listening to the worries and needs of radio journalists. They have been adept at designing hardware and creating software for use by people with technical skills rarely more refined than key-tapping and mouse manipulation.

Figure 7.7 Two sorts of computerised newsroom. Figure 7.7(a) (*above*) shows the BBC local radio Basys system with its list of stories which can be accessed. Figure 7.7(b) (*right*) shows a brave attempt at a paper-less newsroom at Essex FM!

One popular computer network used by some commercial radio stations and the BBC is called Basys. The system receives all news agency wires and incoming copy while journalists key in their stories at local sites which can then be accessed by other regional or national newsrooms. One advantage for local journalists is that they too can access their colleague's work (and contacts) elsewhere so, for example, BBC Essex in Chelmsford can see the stories being worked on for that evening's regional television news programme at Norwich.

Computerised newsrooms consist of two elements – a digital editor and an enhanced word processing system.

Most systems take in data from news suppliers such as IRN in both copy and audio form. The data is filed by category, stored and automatically sorted into specifically designated lists allowing quick scanning of stories. You can rewrite copy and edit audio on screen from a workstation at the same time as data is being filed or updated and other people are also using the same piece of copy or audio. A bulletin editor can 'build' a bulletin on screen, time the total duration and vary the running order up to a tight deadline.

Material can be printed out for reading in the traditional way or alternatively read off screen with audio activated either by a mouse or through a touchscreen. After the bulletin, copy and audio can be archived.

Items from freelancers are automatically brought to the attention of the radio station's accounts department for payment. Most systems also have the storage capacity to contain a comprehensive and updated lists of contacts to which everyone in the newsroom has access.

Computerised newsrooms can also take audio and copy data from digital telephone lines called ISDN circuits (ISDN stands for Integrated Services Digital Network) capable of sending full quality stereo signals via dial-up lines throughout the world. In addition, some bigger newsrooms are equipping reporters with portable audio editing equipment. One system, used by IRN, is called DAVE standing for Digital Audio Visual Editing. It enables on-screen editing in remote locations on equipment no larger than a big suitcase which can then be hooked up to the central newsroom computer intake via ISDN, fax machine or satellite uplink.

'Virtual' news bulletins

An even more revolutionary way of using new technology is through the creation of 'virtual' news bulletins. Some commercial stations are experimenting with this concept where a complete news bulletin is played out from computer.

Each story – either in copy form or a cue 'attached' to a cut – is read by a news presenter as it is prepared and stored individually as a separate file on the computer. The bulletin is constructed from the list of files and turned into one 'play' list. This list of pre-recorded individual stories is then played out one after the other and, because of the use of the newsreader, becomes a complete bulletin. Devices exist for recording and inserting last-minute, breaking stories.

To many traditional journalists, recording news bulletins in any way is anathema; news is always live. However, the 'virtual' bulletin is particularly useful and efficient in situations where a company operates an FM and an AM station; instead of airing one live bulletin on both stations, a separate bulletin can be pre-recorded and played out for AM with a separate editorial agenda reflecting the different target audience.

Studios

A radio studio uses a number of sources of sound. These can include:

- microphones
- CDs

- tapes and cartridges
- digital hard disk
- telephone lines

A studio mixing desk allows all these sources to be combined into a broadcast signal and sent to the transmitter. Which sources are present depends on the purpose of the studio.

A news studio will need a minimum of one microphone. The traditional way of operating is to have a microphone turned on ('opened') and turned off ('closed') from elsewhere (a 'control room') where the technical operator can also mix a newsreader's voice with other sources.

This system has largely been replaced by a more complex news studio, intended to be operated by the news presenter throughout.

This modern news studio contains at least one microphone, a cartridge playing stack (probably a three-slot type known as a triple-stack) and a small mixing desk to combine these sources on air. In more modern stations with digital technology, the cartridge stack will have been replaced by a computer playout system activating audio stored on hard disk by a touchscreen, mouse or keypad.

Figure 7.8 The on-air studio at BBC Essex, Chelmsford, with presenter Dave Monk and Helpline Coordinator Alison Hartley (*right*) and guests. Note the Studer open reel machines in foreground and the increasing use of computer screens

A better equipped studio will also have more microphones, a recording input for the cartridges or to record and store directly onto hard disk, an open-reel tape recorder, a telephone balancing unit and a means of bringing a landline or ISDN link into the output (Figure 7.8).

Such a studio can be used not only for live bulletins but also for recording interviews, recording carts and onto disk (either from the telephone or tape recorder), conducting telephone interviews, recording packages and editing either on open-reel tape or on-screen. A second microphone also makes a live voicer much easier, using a reporter in the studio with the bulletin presenter.

The choice of microphones for news will be fairly narrow, with a number of proven types tending to dominate the market. They include the Beyer M201 and AKG D202 which are all high-performance, directional types. An omnidirectional microphone is not a good choice for a news studio; it will tend to pick up stray noise from unwanted sources. Many news studios – especially in commercial radio – now include an audio processor to help boost the 'punchiness' of the sound not only from the microphones but also other sound sources to make the output sound more consistent. A directional microphone, however, is much more critical from which to keep the right distance – too far away and you will sound weak and distant, too close and you will 'pop' the microphone and sound muffled.

The studio will also contain a telephone balancing unit. These are devices built into a studio mixing desk to allow a telephone call to be brought up as a source on a fader either to be recorded or broadcast live.

Audio and actuality

The 'live' recording of a real event or person is usually called 'audio' in commercial radio and 'actuality' in the BBC. It makes a bulletin sparkle and you should try to use it wherever it is justified.

Audio can be anything from a 17-second cut of the Prime Minister speaking in the Commons to a location interview with the fire chief in charge at a train crash.

Remember, though, that audio should add to a story. Think carefully about what it says and how it will fit into the overall story. Do not use audio just for the sake of it or simply to prove you were there.

Sound quality

Be careful about the technical quality of audio. If it is not good enough, simply do not use it. Try not to feel compelled to use an inferior quality piece of audio just because of the effort which has gone into getting it. Remember that if you have trouble picking out what is being said when you are preparing the audio for transmission in a studio, by the time it reaches a transistor radio, it will make no sense at all.

Audio should be intelligible in itself and capable of being understood at the first hearing. If your listener has to spend two or three seconds trying to guess what is being said, you have failed. It is far better for the story to reach the listener as copy or a voicer rather than use inferior quality audio which cannot be understood.

Sound edits

Listen carefully to your selected piece of audio and make sure every word is essential. Edit out really bad 'ers', 'ums' and stumbles, but be careful not to make the audio seem too unnatural and pay particular attention to making sure edits do not disrupt background noise. Make sure all the edits are 'clean', with the correct breath pauses.

Dubbing

Dubbing means transferring a piece of audio from one recorder to another. This may be from a cassette machine to an open-reel machine in an analogue recording system or from a DAT tape to a computer hard disk for editing in a digital newsroom.

Levels and equalisation

The importance of good audio volume levels cannot be underestimated. It is silly to have spent time and effort preparing a story only to have it unheard by the listener because the volume is either too low or too high and distorted.

When audio is dubbed for playout either on cartridge or computer, it is vitally important that the volume level is correctly set. This is so

Figure 7.9 The PPM meters on a BBC local radio broadcast desk. From left to right, prefade, desk output and station output

that, when it comes to be played in a bulletin or programme, no further adjustments need to be made to be levels.

Levels are measured in the studio by using a peak programme meter or PPM. Different stations have different rules about the level to which audio peaks, but generally you should aim at just over PPM 5 for the loudest sound. Telephone recordings contain a narrower band of frequencies, so the PPM level for phone audio should be slightly higher, to a maximum of PPM 6. The effective volume is then the same (Figure 7.9).

Equalisation controls (EQ) on a studio mixing desk can be either a help or a hazard. They are glorified tone controls similar to but more sophisticated than the bass or treble controls on a domestic stereo system. You can use them, for instance, to remove high frequencies such as tape hiss or the low frequencies of an air conditioning system. They are also used to adjust the tonal qualities of voices. However, you should be careful you know what you are doing; you may end up producing a muffled piece of audio which suffers from the same problem as low or high levels, i.e. the listener cannot hear it properly.

Telephone versus quality audio

There are two theories about the merits of telephone versus quality audio in newsrooms. It has been generally accepted that face-to-face quality audio is better than audio recorded over the phone. Remember it sounds far better to interview with background noise giving atmosphere, such as a busy office, a factory floor or a traffic-clogged street. This gives the impression of being 'busy'. Except where the background noise is excessive, it is hardly ever necessary to 'find a quiet corner' somewhere and record an interview. This will sound simply as if it had been recorded in a studio, which reduces the point of getting audio in the first place.

Phone audio has traditionally been thought of as a lazy and cheap way of doing interviews, avoiding the time and cost of travelling to a location. This is not necessarily the case and there has emerged a clear editorial justification for doing interviews like this.

Research shows that the listener does not mind phone cuts at all. In fact, he or she thinks the story is actually more 'immediate' if it is done on the phone. It sounds to them as if you have reacted fast to a story rather than done something which has required planning, travelling and a lot of time.

So phone audio not only makes use of radio's greatest strength – its immediacy – but also makes good economic sense for small stations with few staff and limited resources.

8

Interviewing

Types of interview

The purpose of an interview is to gather usable audio to illustrate your story. This audio may be live or recorded. If it is recorded – which is more likely – the end result could be 15 seconds or several minutes. The cut itself could be used for a news bulletin, a package or a documentary. In spite of these varied uses, the principles of good interviewing are the same. We interview for a variety of reasons: to expand or explain a story; to give credibility to a story; to follow up a story; to give a right of reply; or to convey feeling and atmosphere. But before you start, you should have a good idea of the type of interview you are about to do and its purpose.

Informational interviews

This is primarily to reveal facts or opinions. For example, 'How many ambulances are off the road because of a maintenance problem?'; 'Which way do you as an MP intend to vote in tonight's crucial Commons vote?'; 'Why weren't the main roads in the county gritted before last night's frost?'

Note some of the words used. The crucial words to use when asking questions are: *who, what, where, why, when* and *how*. Questions starting with these words elicit answers other than just 'yes' or 'no', therefore making them much more useful on radio. They are known as 'open' questions. 'Closed' questions such as, 'Do you think the county's roads were sufficiently gritted last night?' can lead an interviewee simply to say 'yes'. The interview intended to reveal information is most likely to achieve its object if the questions are short and direct but 'open'.

Interpretive interviews

The interpretive interview is quite different. The subject of the interview needs to interpret some facts which are already known. The *fact* is that interest rates are rising again; the financial expert can be asked what *effect* this will have on mortgage rates. You should still, though, ask questions using the word 'what'. In this case, you are no longer dealing with an existing situation; the expert is being asked to look into the future and sketch the probabilities, usually based on knowledge of what has happened in similar circumstances before.

Emotional interviews

The emotional interview is by far the most tricky type. Good reporting covers all shades and colours of human emotional experiences. There is the happiness of the sporting record breaker; the anxiety of a mother whose child is missing; the anger of a man who has been attacked and robbed. In an emotional interview, a certain amount of silence is more telling than any words, as the subject pauses to gather his or her thoughts, perhaps in the midst of mental turmoil.

Journalists are sometimes criticised for exploiting the emotions of others who may be in trouble or despair. In reality, no one can be compelled to talk if they do not wish to, and it has been said that people suffering in some way can find relief in recounting their feelings. After a big train or motorway crash, there is rarely a shortage of survivors who are anxious to tell their stories. It is often suggested by journalists that the act of describing a narrow escape seems to reduce the shock. However, that is not to condone the actions of a small minority of reporters – sometimes from newspapers – who undeniably overstep the bounds of decency in their efforts to get the big 'tear-jerker'. Journalists do not have the licence to cause extra misery to people who are already suffering enough.

Interview preparation

If you are to ask sensible questions, you must know something about the subject. That is not to say that you need to be an expert yourself, but a few minutes of research is important beforehand.

However, you may well get pushed into an interview without any chance to prepare whatsoever. In that case, use your interviewee as a research resource. Let us say you are about to interview a union representative who is calling for a strike. You know little more than his name, his employer's name, and the union he represents. If you ask for an outright briefing before the interview, he may respect your honesty or he may feel contempt for your lack of knowledge, however unavoidable it may have been. So start the recording and ask a wide-ranging question: 'Why do you think that a strike is now inevitable?' It is difficult to answer that question without giving a clue to the last offer from the employer! Now that you know the last offer was an extra 4%, you can go on to ask what would be acceptable and so on. The interview has begun.

Location

You may carry out an interview almost anywhere. Most are recorded, but even live interviews can be conducted in many places outside the traditional studio. When you go out on location, make the most of opportunities which may exist to include location sound when these are relevant. Some well-meaning interviewees will offer you a 'quiet room'. They are rarely of any use unless they are a purpose-built studio. In particular, many rooms in offices and factories can be full of gloss-painted walls and hard metal objects. The resulting recording will sound as if it was made in a swimming bath, full of harsh echo.

The 'quiet' room, even if it is reasonably well furnished and acoustically tolerable, still has one overwhelming defect – it is deadly boring. The point of going out on location is to paint an audio picture for the listener. Our colours are sound and our brush is a microphone, but the principles are the same. So question the airport manager with the sounds of jets taxiing on the tarmac in the background; interview the union representative near the production line; talk to the teacher with children in the playground (if the school bell rings, carry on – it all adds spice!).

If all else fails, simply conduct the interview outside. The combination of birdsong, distant traffic, footsteps, the rustle of trees and similar sounds combine in what is sometimes known as 'atmosphere' or 'atmos' for short. Indeed, there are sound effects CDs consisting of nothing else, which are intended to create a counterfeit exterior background for commercials and plays recorded in studios. Atmos is a curious phenomenon – we simply do not notice it in reality, but it jumps out of the radio!

You need to be aware of the dangers of background sound. Do not let them be too loud or your interview will be drowned. Your interviewee may also be distracted and feel obliged to shout. Do realise that a continuous sound, like traffic, will make seamless editing almost impossible. The background sound will change abruptly at every splice. And do not be tempted to add sounds from effects CDs which are not there! That is not objective reporting. It is acceptable, though, to record some extra background sound after an interview – say 30 seconds of general background without any speech. Known as 'wildtrack', this clean sound can help if an edit is unavoidable, as it can be dubbed into the main recording to cover a splice. It is also useful as a background to your links when putting a wrap or package together.

'What did you have for breakfast?'

This question has gone into the lore of radio reporting. Newcomers – and some old hands – think it helps to ask the interviewee about the first meal of the day in order to get some recording level and get the conversation going. It is all rather artificial and is better avoided – especially after one famous politician answered: 'An interviewer'!

It is much more practical to ask an interviewee for his name and job title. You can take some level on that and your recording is immediately tagged with crucial information. Do not rely on sticky paper labels alone; they can fall off at vital moments.

A chat before the interview is fine – assuming you have the time. It is perfectly acceptable for the interviewee to ask what, in general, the piece will be about, if that is not already obvious. You can do a little more discreet research at the same time. But never allow an interviewee to insist on a list of questions in advance. You cannot let yourself be tied in this way because, by agreeing to ask certain things, you are also agreeing not to raise other matters which may become more interesting as the interview progresses.

Never have an in-depth discussion with the interviewee beforehand.

Often you will get your best material when the recorder is switched off. They are also likely to say: '. . . as I said before . . .' when obviously the listener would not have heard.

Watch the language

Of course everyone should use words acceptable for broadcasting. But there is another kind of language – the language of the body. The interviewee may inadvertently reveal a lot about his mental state by his posture. Folded arms may be a sign of defensiveness; wringing hands, crossed legs and tapping fingers may reveal various states of tension. Tapping fingers, by the way, must be stopped with a courteous request. Otherwise the recording will probably be spoilt by a most peculiar thumping sound. Be careful also about the way you hold the microphone. Do not move your fingers too much or this will be picked up and also remove rings which might scratch against the outer casing of the microphone. It is also easy to shove the microphone under someone's nose which is highly distracting. Try to tuck it neatly under the interviewee's chin (Figure 8.1).

Figure 8.1 Be sure to tuck your microphone under the chin of the interviewee to allow eye contact

Question technique

You encourage an interviewee to talk by asking questions. That is your job. But do not be tempted into dominating the conversation – the listener wants to hear the voice of the interviewee rather than that of the interviewer.

Eye contact

Encourage your subject with eye contact; it is friendly up to a point, but glance elsewhere now and then, otherwise it becomes aggressive. Use nods of the head to show that you are listening and understanding. Do not say 'yes' or 'I see' and other audible means of encouragement we use in conversation. Your words will be a real nuisance when the interview is played back.

If you need to check your audio recorder – to confirm the level or make sure the cassette or DAT is still rolling – then do so, but look back at your subject quickly. The interviewee will be disconcerted if you gaze elsewhere for long. She will think you are bored!

Listening to answers

This is another good argument against prearranged questions. You must listen to what your subject is saying:

SUBJECT: 'So a man of my height, just over six feet six, does have a real problem finding clothes that fit.'

REPORTER: (not listening): 'So how tall are you then?'

Asking one thing at a time

Make an effort *not* to ramble:

REPORTER: 'Would you say, then, that bus drivers have had enough, that is, that they are saying they aren't paid enough so that they might take action – er, actually go on strike?'

Do not ask multiple questions:

REPORTER: 'Is it true that treating the roads cost the county more than thirty thousand pounds last winter and that you had to use salt as well as grit and that it didn't work well in places?'

Do not start quoting alternatives – then stop in mid-sentence:

REPORTER: 'Are you recommending to victims that they go to the police or the council or the Citizens' Advice Bureau or . . . ?'

Try not to interrupt, unless your subject is never going to stop until you intervene. Interruptions often sound untidy, and they are very difficult to edit sensibly into a short cut.

If you are in any doubt about suitable questions, remember the basics: *who, what, where, why, when* and *how*. For example: 'What's happened?'; 'Where's the accident?'; 'Who's involved?'; 'How many people have been injured?'; 'Why did the coach overturn?'; 'When will the road be clear?' There is no particular order of priority. It depends on the circumstances. However this kind of direct questioning will get you information quickly. Then you ask any necessary supplementary questions.

Leading questions

These questions encourage a certain answer and they are useful up to a point for creating the opportunity for an interviewee to say something which may make a good cut. Do not overdo these questions, as you are in danger of putting words into your subject's mouth. Beware also that they are necessarily 'closed' type questions which could lead simply to a 'yes' or 'no' answer: 'So would you say that mothers must take extra care?'; 'You must be very angry about the decision?'

Cliché questions

Think about your question technique. Each question you ask should serve a specific purpose. Do not fall into 'knee-jerk' interviewing habits:

REPORTER (to sobbing woman): 'How do you feel . . . ?'

After the interview

Do not go on longer than is reasonably necessary. Remember that you have got to listen to it all back afterwards. If you want a 30-second cut, 15 minutes is too much to record. Five should be plenty and ten more than ample. If you are after a clip and you hear what you want during the recording, wind up as soon as you can. There is no point in going on in the hope of something better.

Thanks

Remember to thank your subject. It is good public relations, as well as common courtesy, and you might need to talk to them in person again in the future.

Special interviews

Live interviews

Live interviews are difficult, especially when the big story breaks and you need to interview live into the news bulletin. You may have just 60 seconds allocated to a story. Get going quickly. Ask basic questions and keep them very short otherwise you may waste the whole interview on one answer. Concentrate on information. Interruptions may now be unavoidable.

Vox pops

Vox pops – literally the Latin *vox populi* or the voice of the people – are useful for lightweight subjects such as how people celebrate St Valentine's Day, or a breaking story of really universal interest like a rise in income tax.

A good vox pop consists of short statements from members of the public, chosen at random in a street, neatly edited together in a stream of comments. Try to vary your subjects between young and old, male and female. The cue should make it absolutely clear what the question was. Out in the street, stick to that one question and do not be drawn into a long interview with one person. Names of interviewees are not necessary for once – and neither is it necessary to name the reporter.

Here is a sample cue, adapted from a story about a Royal birth: 'Princess Sharon's new baby girl is to be called Tracey Jane Frances Victoria. The choice breaks with traditional as there's never been a member of the Royal Family called Tracey before. We went out on the streets of Southend to see what people think about Princess Tracey . . .'

If there is a clear majority of opinion on a controversial subject, your vox pop should echo that slant. If most people do not like the idea of a princess called Tracey, then most of your clips should express the general opposition. Choose a humorous clip to end, if the subject allows.

Remember that not everyone likes being approached at random by a radio reporter. Keep smiling, keep your recorder rolling, stay courteous and do not pester people who do not want to know. If you are a nuisance, you will bring the name of your radio station into disrepute and you could be 'moved on' by police.

News conferences

These can be a free-for-all. Some are relatively well organised in a hall or conference room – even a church. Others are impromptu affairs on a doorstep, which start when a VIP emerges from a meeting. Do not be afraid to be at the front of the scrum. You and your microphone have just as much right as any other reporter. Television crews may not appreciate having your microphone in their shot – that is their tough luck. On the other hand, do not deliberately block their view with the back of your head.

If the VIP is going to say something once and disappear, you need the story just as much as anyone else, so be firm with any of your professional colleagues who try to elbow you out of the centre of the story because you are 'only local radio'. Sadly, there are a few reporters who may try this, claiming they are more important. Do not be intimidated. In this game, everyone is equal.

At more organised news conferences, do not hesitate to request one-on-one interview facilities. The organisers may be genuinely ignorant of radio's needs and suppose that questions shouted from the body of the hall will be adequate, as they can be for newspaper journalists. It is acceptable to 'share' or 'pool' recorded interviews on these occasions, if necessary. All radio reporters record at the same time and each one should get in a question or two. Do not worry if the result is a mixture of questioning voices, including reports from 'the opposition'. Consult your editor, naturally, but as a general rule, such interviews are dramatic and deserve a good piece of airtime.

Unattended studios

These are common in local radio and are frequently situated in civic centres and other public buildings in towns distant from the radio station. The unattended studio (sometimes called a 'remote' studio) is linked to the main station by landline or ISDN line which gives good quality speech reproduction.

The radio station often asks an interviewee to go to the studio, let themselves in and turn on the equipment so they can be interviewed 'down the line'. There is always a microphone, a phone and usually some form of simple mixer. There should be clear, understandable instructions about what needs to be switched on and what phone number should be called so that the interviewee can alert the newsroom to his arrival.

The interview itself is conducted using the quality line to carry the subject's voice to the radio station. Questions are usually asked via the phone. If the questions are recorded simultaneously at the radio station end by the reporter through her own microphone, the result is a full 'quality' interview, even though the two parties may be 20 or more miles apart.

9

News reporting

The radio reporter

The traditional image of the reporter is of a scruffy figure in a trenchcoat, foot in the door, notebook in hand, demanding 'What have you got to hide?' or 'The public has a right to know.' If such reporters exist, there is no place for them in radio. Radio reporters do not threaten or browbeat, they do not resort to deceit or bribes. They also look smart as they never know where they might be sent. The Prime Minister will not want to be interviewed by a scruffbag!

The job of the reporter is to get the information or audio, get it right and get it on the radio – fast. Radio reporters know where to go to get the information, and who to talk to. They have an instinctive 'nose for news', ask lots of questions, are boundlessly enthusiastic and never give up until they have what they want.

A reporter also needs a touch of scepticism and suspicion. He or she accepts little at face value and sometimes realises that lurking behind a chance remark, a single fact, a few obscure sentences, an official silence, there may be a great deal more to be revealed.

Nowadays, it is usually the BBC and the larger commercial stations who employ full-time reporters. In medium-sized and smaller commercial stations, reporters are expected to combine their skills with news presenting, bulletin editing and writing. Reporting is only one aspect of the job. But, of all the journalist's skills, it is probably the most essential.

The briefing

All good reporters do their homework before going out on a story. It is useless for a reporter to be following up a story without knowing background information. You should keep fully informed and check cuttings and previous stories, if available. To a certain extent, the newsdesk will be able to brief you when assigning you to a story. This may take the form of a complete file of previous stories, or may simply be a name, address or phone number. Whatever, it is essential to think laterally and gather as much information as possible, within the timescale, before actually going out on the road.

Remember, driving time is good thinking time (within the bounds of road safety!). While you are driving to the story, think about what you want to achieve, what is expected of you and how you are going to tackle the subject. For a moment, go back to basics, and ask yourself: 'What is this story *really* about?'

Fixing ahead

There are two different sorts of reporting jobs. The first is a diary assignment – a function, event or interview notified to the newsdesk in advance, usually by a press release or phone call. For this, you need to arm yourself with the relevant background papers, read them and then, the most important thing of all, *think*.

You will usually be told (though sometimes it is up to you to decide) how much material is required and in what form. For example, a launch of a new counselling service for people suffering from depression may produce a 35-second bulletin wrap, a cut or clip alternative and a four-minute package for a programme.

You will also be told when the various pieces are required. You could be sent out at 2pm and told something is needed for the 4pm news. Or, if it is not so important, the piece would simply be an 'overnight' for the next morning.

On this sort of job, most of the information about where and when to turn up is made available in advance. Sometimes a phone call is needed if you have particular interview or audio needs.

The other sort of job is the instant reaction callout. A bomb has exploded, a fire has started or a police officer has been shot. There is little time to think or plan ahead. You simply get to the scene as quickly as possible and tell the story. If it is a big story requiring live coverage, your newsdesk will need not only to despatch you with the radio car but, in addition, arrange permission for access and parking.

Working to deadlines

It is important that you as the reporter know what your newsdesk needs and when it needs it. The deadline is vital. It is no use having a brilliant clip of audio of a stunning eyewitness account of an event if it misses the bulletin. Know what is needed before you leave the newsroom. Ironically, you will find that you work better having a deadline and being put under pressure.

In a major incident, it is important to stay in touch with the newsdesk as much as possible so that you can be told of changes in deadlines and requirements. News is all about what is happening now. Your deadline could be five minutes before a bulletin or it could be while the bulletin is on the air as you do a live insert from a mobile phone or radio car. Whatever it is, make sure you stick to the deadline and file something – anything – by that time.

On location

The big story has broken, you have been briefed, told of your deadlines, researched any background, grabbed photocopies of previous stories, remembered to take a mobile phone (and switch it on!), remembered to grab your portable audio recorder (with microphone, recharged batteries and tape!) and you are on your way through the traffic to the story, all the time thinking about what to do, how to do it and how to get the story on the air. You will be listening to your station's output, or that of your rivals, to glean as much up-to-date information being put out as possible.

What to do first

On arrival at the scene of the fire, explosion, shooting or whatever, you have first to assess the situation. Find out if the event is still happening or has finished. Make contact with the emergency services. Try to grab an interview with the police officer or fire chief in charge straightaway. If it is a dramatic event which is still continuing, phone the newsdesk

Figure 9.1 Essex FM Head of News Peter Stewart interviewing an
eyewitness using a portable Sony cassette recorder

immediately. File a 'holding' voicer from the scene, describing what
you can see. After you have done this, ask your newsdesk to contact
the emergency services and find out who is in charge and enlist their
co-operation. Then turn on your portable recorder and start recording
background noise or 'wildtrack' for later use in wraps and packages.
Record at least a couple of minutes. If there are explosions, sirens or
shots, keep the recorder rolling.

Describe what is happening as you can see it and hear it. It does
not matter is this appears to sound like rubbish at first; just keep recording
and talking without making a judgement and you may be surprised at the
results of your commentary and what you will eventually be able to use.

Eyewitness accounts

Usually at these incidents there are bystanders watching what is
going on. Try to find an eyewitness to the incident you are reporting.

Keep the recorder rolling. Make sure you identify yourself, but get them talking in front of a microphone. Most people are only too happy to describe what they saw and what they did and thought. You only need to a few seconds of the most dramatic account. Ask questions. Do not forget, at the end, to get their name and record it on your portable (Figure 9.1).

Dealing with officials

The emergency services have a job to do. Theirs is the most important job, not yours. They are in the business, in many cases, of saving lives. Let them get on with it. Try not to get in the way. However, watch out for the fire fighters who are resting or police officers who are waiting and watching, and try to get instant reactions and descriptions from them. Of course, this will not always work and you will sometimes be told in no uncertain terms to go away.

In general, deal with the senior officers. If there is a press officer on the scene (which usually happens in major incidents), make sure he or she knows who you are and what you need. They will usually organise an on-the-spot briefing from a senior officer. Make sure you know where and when this is being held and if there are plans for regular updates.

Always keep in touch with the newsdesk via your mobile phone and tell them what is happening. Keep filing your eyewitness accounts and from-the-scene voicers.

Dealing with other reporters

It is up to you whether you associate with the scores of other television, radio and newspaper reporters who will turn up at a dramatic event. Usually it is best to work in a group and help each other out, although always be on the lookout for the exclusive eyewitness that the others have failed to spot.

It helps to pool information, especially official information, to make sure everyone is broadcasting the same facts. Facts are sacred and not exclusive. Views, comment and interpretation can be up to you.

Filing material

Once you have arrived at the scene of a dramatic news story, it is important to get something on the air as soon as possible.

Figure 9.2 Working with the radio van used for live broadcasting by Essex FM and The Breeze

Getting on the air

Of course, the telephone is the best way of getting a story on the radio quickly. The most flexible phone to use in these circumstances is a mobile. If you have to use a payphone, get connected through the operator, reverse the charges and ask the operator to silence the pips, saying you are working for a radio station. Beware that on some payphones, it is impossible to silence the pips and incoming calls cannot be accepted. If you are covering a siege or other story which requires you to stay close to what is going on and you do not have access to a mobile or payphone, knock on a few doors and see if there is a person willing to let you use their phone.

By far the best way of getting on the air with quality audio, though, is by using a radio car with a UHF transmitter. Radio car facilities vary from station to station but, in essence, they are simply a way of connecting a microphone and recorder to a mini mixer and sending the signal back to base via a big aerial. The aerial is raised by a small electrical pump but it is vital to ensure that there are no overhead obstructions such as power or telephone cables before pressing the 'up' button. Once the link is established, the studio can receive audio and voicers in quality and either broadcast them live or record them for editing and later transmission. Some BBC stations are now equipped

Figure 9.3 Senior Journalist Tim Gillet broadcasting live from the BBC Essex radio van. Note the telescopic transmitting aerial in the centre

with larger radio vans with enhanced facilities for self-contained outside broadcasts of speech programmes (Figures 9.2 and 9.3).

On-the-spot voicers

If something dramatic is happening, try to ad-lib your report. This will convey the drama of the event. If you have time, script your piece or work from notes. Some radio stations now equip their reporters with mini word processors which help in these circumstances. If you cannot type your words, make sure your handwriting is clear. Many reporters have come to an embarrassing silence midway through a report because they cannot read their own scrawl! Try to sound dramatic, but do not go over the top and 'ham it up' too much. Do not shout, but sound forceful. End with a standard outcue or SOC, for example: 'Terry Lawrence, BBC News, Dover' or whatever your own station style requires.

Live reports and Q-and-As

Usually your piece will be pre-recorded. Sometimes it is better and more dramatic to do a live piece into a bulletin or programme. Make sure you can hear the off-air cue properly down the phone. Be sure to know when you will be needed and for how long. Try to get in a position where background noise can be heard. Again, remember the rules about working from a script if possible.

Question-and-answer pieces (also known as 'Q-and-As' or 'two-ways') happen when a presenter questions a reporter from the scene. If you are a reporter, make sure you are fully informed and up to date about what is happening. Try not to waffle just for the sake of it. Give the facts and do not speculate. Be responsible in what you say. Remember that in a siege, for example, a gunman could possibly have a radio tuned to your station and be listening as you describe the position of the police firearms team. If this is the case, you will not be able to tell your listener the whole story. You are there to report what is happening, not to influence it.

Q-and-As should be planned where possible, but if you are asked something about which you do not know the answer, be honest and say so.

'Car park' voicers

In certain circumstances, it can help to enliven a script or story by recording it outside, maybe in your station's car park on a portable recorder rather than in a studio. It is an effective production technique which creates an impression of being on the spot. However – do not claim in your standard outcue that you are on location. One day you will be caught out!

Production

Once you have arrived back in the newsroom, having filed all your phone or radio car pieces from site, you begin the daunting task of trying to put all the material together. On big stories, you will be required to assemble at least one short bulletin piece and a longer programme package from what could be as much as 45 minutes' worth of pre-recorded material such as interviews and background sound.

Remember you are crafting a piece, like an artist. Radio is theatre of the mind and you have to be creative when using words and sounds.

Choosing the cut

Remember the different ways of getting something on the air. You are probably first of all looking for an audio cut – a 20- or 25-second piece from an interview. Secondly, you are listening for an alternative cut and, thirdly, you need to wrap everything together. Do not forget the immense value of listening to everything you have recorded, in order to begin the selection process, on the way back to the newsroom from the scene while you are in a car or taxi. It saves valuable editing time if you can walk into the newsroom with a clear idea of what you are able to deliver and start editing and dubbing work straightaway.

Choose the most dramatic quotes from the audio you have gathered. Use the audio to get across descriptions, opinion or interpretations. Concentrate on the facts in the cue. Do not edit so tightly that the audio sounds unnatural, and make the cuts long enough to register with the listener. A cut of just three seconds is easily missed.

Choose a cut that has a proper start and ends properly – in other words, a self-contained statement. Do not choose a cut which starts 'But . . .' or 'Well . . .' (if you can help it). Try as far as possible to exclude your own voice. As you become more practised, you will develop an 'ear' for a cut, as soon as your interviewee says it, while recording. Always spend time 'cleaning' the audio. If the interviewee stumbles too much, the whole point is lost.

Wrapping or packaging

To construct your wrap or package, you will first of all need to listen to all your audio and make notes about what bits you want to use. Choose the cuts you want, then the wildtrack or background sounds. Dub them onto individual carts or put them in separate computer audio files. Label the carts and files carefully so they can easily be identified. Write your script, then go to the production studio and record the whole wrap in one go onto either an open reel tape recorder or onto another computer file. You can tighten up the audio if necessary later on.

There is another method of putting a package together and this is the technique of recording everything onto tape or computer hard disk in the order you need it, including your voice, and then editing it all together. This is more time consuming and gives you less flexibility for using individual audio cuts in other pieces later.

Be sure to know exactly what is wanted from you. By this, you should know whether it is for a bulletin or programme and how long it is supposed to be. You also need a deadline.

Try to make as much use of audio and background sounds as you can. After all, sound is what radio is all about. Once again, this is a creative process. Show your sound off. The more the listener feels he or she is at the scene, the better. You can add impact to your piece by starting it with a cut of an interviewee or the sound of something happening. And do not forget the value of using music as background or as a 'stager' at the start of your wrap; after all, music is the staple diet of many stations and it is a powerful way to connect to a listener.

Writing cues

Do not include anything in your pre-recorded wrap or package which is likely to be out of date by the time it is broadcast, otherwise this will ensure you have the headache of a last-minute editing job. Make sure there is space for this information to be included in the cue.

It is particularly important, when material is coming in to a bulletin or programme editor at breakneck speed, to make sure all the technical information about duration and outcue is included and marked clearly on both the cue itself, the cart or the computer file stored for playout. In particular, ensure that your piece is correctly timed.

10

Newsdesk management

The newsdesk is the centre of the news operation. Information arrives in a varying flow, depending on the time of day. Peak times tend to be the early morning up to the 8am bulletins (which on the vast majority of stations attracts the biggest audience of the day as people get ready for work); again in the hour up to 1pm and once more in the early evening from 4pm. A big, breaking story can quickly generate numerous audio clips and a mountain of copy.

Running the newsdesk

Getting organised with paper and tape

An untidy newsdesk can be a nightmare. The best stories can be mislaid at the last, crucial moment in a pile of disorganised copy.

So run a newsdesk as you would a military operation. In newsrooms still using paper and tape, plastic office trays are good to contain copy as well as suitable racks for carts. Copy paper can be either A4 or A5, but the smaller size is easier to handle. At least one carbonless copy is useful.

One tray is for current bulletin material. Some bulletin editors like to assemble the next bulletin in skeleton form at the front of such a tray, adding to it as the minutes go by. In the last 15 minutes, it is helpful to have some space to lay out the growing bulletin story by story so that late items can be inserted in their appropriate places right up to the last possible moment.

Another tray should contain stories from earlier in the same day which have been used and superseded. Do not let old copy stray too far – something in it could be needed to update a running story ('. . . just how many jobs are there at that company? We were quoting that figure this morning . . .'), and the contents of the 'used' tray will form the overnight 'clip up' – the daily file of stories kept for reference.

If there is room, further trays can hold the cues for the national audio, if you use it, and also freelance copy.

Organising carts

The cart rack can be organised in whatever way suits you best, but it can be useful to keep local and national carts in two separate sequences. Clips from the BBC's GNS have catchlines or 'slugs'; IRN audio cuts are numbered; labelling the carts with the IRN number and keeping them in order saves valuable seconds.

Proper cart labelling is very important. Inadequate information can lead to the wrong cart being played on air. A label should show the catchline of the story – preferably just one word – as well as the name of the person speaking (or name of the reporter for a voicer), the duration and outcue (the last two or three words so that the news presenter knows when it ends and can continue smoothly). For example:

COMMONS/Blair act
23" OUT: ...they were in power

STRIKE/Chantler voicer
28" OUT:...early next week

There are various conventions for cart labelling. Different stations have their own habits, but generally 'fx' means a sound effect:

OUT .... (laughter fx)

If a word or phrase is said more than once, the repetition is shown as follows:

OUT ... their problem (x2)

The (x2) means that the news presenter will wait to hear that phrase twice before carrying on. Some stations use (rpt.) for the same purpose, but that does not cater for a word turning up three times – it can happen.

Another abbreviation is 'act' for actuality – meaning a clip of an event, interview or speech, but not a reporter's voice.

Getting organised with computers

Needless to say, it is usually easier to organise a computerised newsroom than a traditional one simply because many of the functions of organisation, such as archiving and sorting, can be established and triggered automatically.

There are a growing number of different software systems being designed and used for newsrooms, however most share a common way of handling cues and cuts.

There will be a template for writing cues and copy. All you have to do is fill in the blanks for catchline and the body of the cue or copy. It will probably be automatically dated, numbered and timed for you as you write. After preparing the story, you file it ready for broadcast. If you are the bulletin editor, you can call up a list or menu of stories ready for use, read and correct them if necessary and re-order them either for printing if you wish to handle paper or for cueing on the playout machine in the news studio ready for you to read on air from the screen. After use, the stories can be archived under date and time.

New technology now exists for news suppliers such as IRN to download their material directly into your computer system. This is relatively straightforward for copy stories, which appear as a menu like that for local stories, but is more complicated for audio owing to the lack of an agreed 'labelling' system.

Taking audio

The news supplier will 'feed' audio at regular intervals, although news does not operate to a schedule and a cut can easily turn up outside these times. This means you should keep a constant ear on the supplier's output. Have some clean carts ready – newsdesks find lengths of 20, 35, 40 and maybe 50 inches most useful. With a computer, set up an automatic alert system which 'flags' a symbol on screen when a supplier sends a new story or piece of audio.

In analogue newsrooms, it is best to cart up the audio directly from the feed, but keep the logger tape running too. If you miss one, you can always run the tape back and dub it to the cart, but this takes more time.

Carts, when played, should always start clean, with neither a long pause nor a 'clipped' front. A cart should be started ('fired') just *before* the audio to allow the recording cart machine to come up to speed. BBC stations have an advantage: GNS provides a cart firing pulse at the front of news clips they feed.

In computer newsrooms, always check the audio stored before playout. You may want to 'tidy' up a piece of audio using the waveform digital editor. The same rules for labelling audio apply to computer systems as carts and tapes.

Deadlines

Be ruthless about deadlines. Put into effect a 'gate' so that five minutes before a bulletin, you can 'close' it to new material and go into the studio. If you are on your own in the newsroom, do not worry about that updated audio which arrives two minutes to the hour. You cannot be in the newsroom carting it and reading the bulletin in the studio simultaneously; and you might miss the start of a bulletin for the sake of one update, which would be a disaster. The bulletin matters most. In the end, the listener is probably only listening to one radio station and he or she does not know what stories you have failed to carry. But the listener will notice if the bulletin sounds odd and breathless or is not there at all!

Bulletin construction

Finding the lead

Having a tidy and well-organised newsdesk means that you can see what stories are available and you can then move on to the next step – putting the bulletin together.

The first decision is to choose the lead story. The lead will be the most important story – the one which, in your judgement, will be the most likely to grab the listener's attention. Some leads choose themselves – the Prime Minister resigning, or hundreds of people dying in a plane crash, or the Russians just landing a man on Mars!

But there are other days when there is no obvious top story. In this case, choose the best three or four, those that 'sound like leads', and cycle them in different bulletins. There is no rule that says the top two stories in the 10am bulletin should not be reversed for the 11am. However, the first words of the bulletin should be fresh. This may mean re-writing a story with a new cue, so go ahead and do it. What does sound bad is the 'lead' story which turned up in exactly the same form as the second story in the previous bulletin.

If you are looking for leads, pay close attention to the most recent TV news or bulletins on other radio stations, or even (especially in the early morning) what the newspapers are doing. There are limits to this; the tabloids may lead with a vicar-and-blonde-in-a-sex-romp story which is probably unsuitable for your station. If all the nationals agree on a lead (which is not that common), then they are probably correct. Remember, though, that they wrote their stories several hours ago – look for an angle which will update the news for the breakfast audience.

One more point: if your bulletins are 'mixes' of national and local stories, do not be afraid to lead with a local news when you can. A strike involving 200 people in a local factory may be more important in your area than a bigger industrial dispute elsewhere. Some stations lead with local stories as a matter of policy, but critics of this say rigid rules about local versus national can result in distorted bulletin priorities.

The rest of the bulletin

Stories in the rest of the bulletin are often easier to put in order once your lead is established. There is no shame in simply running copy stories. In fact, many stations insist on a high 'copy story count' as this improves the pace of a bulletin.

If there is a major story which dominates most of the bulletin with several cuts of audio and voicers, acknowledge the others by saying '. . . in other news . . .' then do a couple of lines on each.

Try to avoid using the same introductory phrase again and again. Even though there is nothing wrong with it, a constant stream of 'Here's a report from . . .' is unimaginative and can have a soporific effect on the listener. Use phrases like 'David Bull explains why . . .', James Edwards outlines the problems involved . . .', 'Kevin Jones was told the full details of what happened.' When there is a reporter in court, say so 'Nick Rogers was in court.' However, beware of clumsy phrasing: 'In court was our reporter Nick Rogers!'

In the intro to each cut, ensure the listener is prepared for any distracting background noises. A line in the cue which says Tim Page spoke to the councillor in a busy canteen will prevent the listener being overly distracted by the clinking of crockery and will enable concentration on what is actually being said.

Each story should be self-contained. As far as possible within the constraints of brevity, your listener should not need to know what was reported yesterday to understand what is being said today.

Remember that stories about the same general subject should be linked ('. . . and still on the subject of house prices . . .'). This is called creating an 'umbrella' of stories by topic, theme or thread. It works well if, in a mixed bulletin, you can follow a national piece with a local angle on the same story. Try to end with what is called a 'kicker' – something light, curious or genuinely funny (note the word 'genuinely'!) – as this makes for an easier transition into general programming from the news, but do not fret if there is nothing like that around. Try recapping the lead story again if your station does not forbid it: '. . . and the main story again this hour . . .'. This recapping has a pleasantly urgent ring to it, and also helps the listener who tuned in just after the start. If you do use a kicker, though, remember that it can only be used once.

Follow that story . . . !

Once you have carried a good story, do not let it lie down and die too quickly. Nothing sounds odder than a lead which unaccountably disappears from the next bulletin entirely. Move a story slowly down in successive bulletins before dropping it and keep your story fresh with rewrites. A story which had good audio can be run as copy only later in the day. Should a good new angle develop, your story might well move up again. A story further down the bulletin can be dropped for an hour or two and then brought back. Watch, too, your balance of local, national and international news. A good mixed bulletin should contain all three, but in varying amounts depending on what is going on.

Flash that snap . . . !

A really good, dramatic and unfolding story may not wait for the next scheduled new bulletin. A 'snap' usually becomes a 'newsflash' on air. Keep snaps short, only run them when news is really 'hot', and try not to break a story within a few minutes of the bulletin unless it is top priority. A decision on whether to snap should be taken by the Editor, but it is the Bulletin Editor's responsibility to be on the alert for breaking stories and refer them upwards if necessary.

Other newsdesk duties

The network

It is your local station's job to contribute to the network when a good story breaks locally. Where stations carry the national bulletin live, there is often a clash of interests.

A local story given to the network too quickly may turn up in the national bulletin and eclipse the local news which follows. This is a difficult situation, and one argument in favour of mixed bulletins. Some stations with a really good local story often mix their bulletins 'on demand', so that local listeners do not hear an excellent local story broken by a national newsreader.

In a very competitive radio market where several 'rival' local stations overlap each other's areas and they all take the same national news supply, it is even more of a tricky decision to decide what, if anything, to give to the network. This is because the network gives instant access to your hard-won audio to your opposition. Be careful. Matters such as this need policy decisions by editors in consultation with station management and often depend on the politics of the marketplace.

Check calls

You may be working in a very small newsroom but one vital job which cannot be neglected, if you are to keep the flow of news coming, is regular check calls to the emergency services. The police, fire and ambulance control rooms expect calls from the media, but since not everyone in these services is equally willing to pass on information (some police officers especially remember the days when they were instructed 'don't tell the press anything'), it is wide to cross-check with all the services. In addition, the police may be called to a fire but they may not think it worth mentioning unless someone dies or its looks like arson. The fire service control, on the other hand, is more likely to give details of any callout, serious or not.

An up-to-date 'calls list' is an essential (Figure 10.1). All the emergency services have specialist officers for the press and, as we

POLICE	
Devon and Cornwall HQ	52101
Dorset HQ	01202 220991
Dorset press line	0426 932 435
Avon & Somerset Yeovil	01935 752911
HQ	0117 92 7777
Roads	01225 94567
Barnstaple control	01271 739 111
Paignton control	01803 192011

Local police stations	
Ashburton	01364952211
Bideford	01237 868896
Bridport	01308 224466
Budleigh Salterton	954141
Crediton	01363 922000
Dartmouth	01803 132288
Exeter Heavitree Rd	910199 (ask for duty inspector only)
Exmouth	01395 14653
Honiton	01404 121177
Ivybridge	01752 89567
Newton Abbot	01626 594444
Okehampton	01837 220011
Sidmouth	01395 512666
Teignmouth	01626 743311
Tiverton	01884 523523
Torquay	01803 144911 (ask for station officer)

FIRE	
Devon	871199
Devon press line	0426 122030
Dorset	01305 555911 (urgent calls only)
Somerset press line	01823 199011

AMBULANCE	
Devon (Exeter)	433133
Devon (Torquay)	01803 610922
Dorset	01202 966899
Somerset	01823 889922

COASTGUARD	
Brixham (South Devon)	01803 182344
Portland (East Devon)	01305 161149

Figure 10.1 A typical calls list

mentioned earlier, there are the media voicebank phone lines available to newspaper and television as well as radio journalists. Listen to them as often as possible, preferably once an hour at peak times and before major bulletins.

Headlines and teasers

Depending on your station's policy, you will need to write headlines for putting on air at half past the hour or at other headline break times. These headlines must be no more than two sentences on each story and be completely self-contained. It is rarely possible simply to use the top two lines of the main story. Write fresh headlines for each story. It is a good idea to make it a rule for each reporter filing a story to write a headline which can be stored and used if required. Many stations also like their music presenters to promote and 'tease' the news bulletins. This is an excellent habit to cultivate and is well worth the extra effort to put something together which can be used. For this, you need to supply a taster of what is coming up in the form of, say, the top local story and the top national story. Again, write these fresh from the original story.

Allocating reporters

If you are lucky, you may have one or more reporters available to follow up running stories. They are an expensive resource, so use them with care. Ask yourself whether it is more effective to send someone out on a single story which may take most of the morning or give them several stories to chase from the newsroom, relying on phone or down-the-line interviews. The correct answer could be either option; it all depends on the merits of individual stories.

Giving orders

The Newsdesk Producer (BBC) or Bulletin Editor (commercial radio) has a relatively senior job. It follows that reporters will be taking orders. Producers, therefore, should remember that people respond better to requests rather than demands. It is the Producer's job to make the story clear to the reporter as far as possible. If you, as Producer, have a particular angle in view, do not expect the reporter to read your mind.

However, a good reporter, even if well briefed, will still be on the watch for other angles and may come back with something quite unexpected. It may not have been the way you saw the story initially, but do not be too quick to criticise. After all, the reporter on the spot should be better placed to judge a story. If that judgement really was in error, follow it up calmly later on, having made the best of what you were given at the time. Nothing is worse than a big row about what should have been (but now cannot) be done before you have to present a bulletin!

Priorities

Sometimes a quiet news day can explode with action and drama with several apparently good stories breaking almost simultaneously. If that happens, stand back, keep calm and consider what to do first. Do not over-react and leap at the first thing to hand, because first may not be best. You must weigh up each potential story. Generally pursue the easier ones first. You may get two or three finished in a short time. Then concentrate on the more difficult and time-consuming possibilities. It is a mistake to let everything else drop for the sake of one attractive but elusive story. You could end up with nothing.

Coping with crisis

Occasionally the pace goes on warming up until it is too hot for comfort. If a spectacular story breaks, you do have to let other things go, albeit reluctantly. Consider that if County Hall is on fire with 2,000 council staff evacuated and the town centre sealed off, you will not have time in your bulletins for much else anyway.

Do not hesitate to call for help within the radio station itself. People who are not journalists are nevertheless excellent at staffing the phones when, say, a foot of snow brings your area to a standstill. Staff from the Managing Director's office or the sales room are often intrigued at a chance to 'have a go' at news, even if it is under strict supervision.

Allocate your real journalists with care, pursue the major angles first and always think in terms of the next bulletin – preferably the next two or three. Save one or two items just in case there is no time to get them later on. And do not overlook what is going out live – get a recorder running on the output if the story has spilt over into general programming.

On air in a crisis when reporting a diasaster, one of the major concerns is to prevent distress. You have a responsibility to ensure that no listener is needlessly alarmed. At the beginning of a disaster story, you should try to give all the details of time and place which will help isolate the circumstances of the accident. For example, in the case of a collision between two trains, you should say where it happened, the routes of the trains and their starting point departure times. When reporting accidents to public transport vehicles in large towns or cities, you should try and locate them as precisely – and as early in the story – as possible. The name of the hospital to which casualties have been taken is also helpful together with any emergency phone number released by the police for casualty inquiries.

11

Legalities

Journalists do not have special rights under the law, except for a few occasions when a journalist has a legal right of access which is denied to the public – for example, at a youth court. In addition, some journalists have tested their traditionally proclaimed right to protect their sources, but not always with success. Generally, the journalist has the same rights and responsibilities as any citizen.

It is vital for all radio journalists to have a working knowledge of certain key areas of the law. There is room here for only a brief summary. You can read more detail in McNae's *Essential Law for Journalists* by Tom Welsh and Walter Greenwood (Butterworths).

To stay within the law demands a knowledge of the legal process and of the constraints which the law imposes. The two main areas which concern journalists are *libel* and *contempt*.

The laws of libel and contempt are complex and change from time to time. There are also a number of exceptions to the general rules. If in doubt, take legal advice or consult a specialist book on the subject – before the broadcast!

Libel

The law says everyone has a right to a 'good name' throughout their lives, unless and until there is undeniable evidence to the contrary by, for example, being convicted of a crime.

You should not broadcast anything which would 'expose a person to hatred, ridicule or contempt, cause him to be shunned or avoided, or tend to injure him in his office, trade or profession'.

Anything published which damages someone's reputation is potentially *defamatory*. Defamation is divided into slander (spoken) and libel (published). All broadcast defamation is defined as libel because broadcast speech is more wide-ranging than normal speech and is effectively published, because it is on the radio.

The other difference between slander and libel is that someone must normally suffer injury (for example, by losing their job) as a result of slander in order to win damages. There are a few exceptions to this general rule, but slander will rarely if ever trouble the radio journalist. So far as libel is concerned, mere proof of defamation is enough to win the case. The actual amount awarded, of course, can vary from trivial to extortionate.

To be upheld, libel can only be committed against a clearly identifiable individual or group. It is not possible to defame the dead. Beware, though, because a group of people can be libelled without individual names being used. For example, 'Tory councillors in Blankshire are lining their own pockets as all the council's contracts go to their friends.' This is a plain accusation of a corrupt practice. Any Conservative councillor in Blankshire could claim libel damages.

Libel defences

The best defence

The best defence to libel is not to commit it in the first place. Remember that the comments of interviewees are not just their responsibility. You take on some of the blame by broadcasting them. Be on your guard for what people say.

Truth

The next best complete defence is that what has been said is true. In law, truth is properly called 'justification'. Truth has to be proved to the satisfaction of a jury. However, there are some cases on record where someone has won damages even though the statements were accurate. This is because a listener could have drawn a defamatory conclusion from the way the facts were presented. The conclusions drawn by a reasonable person can certainly change if some facts are left out, for example.

Fair comment

It is possible to defend a libel action by pleading 'fair comment'. This means the views expressed were honestly held and made in good faith without malice. A defence has to show that the remarks were based on demonstrable facts not misinformation.

Criticism is an essential part of the political and democratic process and is not necessarily libellous even if it descends to abuse, although you need to be alert. For example: 'Tory policies in Blankshire are hard-hearted and selfish. The poorest people in the community will once again be the losers while the rich will get richer. It's the same old miserable story of Damn You, Jack, I'm All Right.'

In the context of a reasonable debate, this is not a libellous statement. It is considered fair comment on a matter of public interest and it is legally acceptable for people to express honest opinions and beliefs.

Despite there being no legal liability, you should give the Conservative group in Blankshire a chance to put their point of view in the interest of balance.

Be aware that some other words are potentially libellous and you should be careful how they are used and in what context. One of these is the word 'cruel'. Allegations of cruelty should be made only after very careful consideration. Also, make good use of the words 'claim' and 'allegation' in any story likely to prove controversial and critical of someone.

Privilege

Another defence is that the libellous words reported were covered by 'privilege'. There are two sorts of privilege. Absolute privilege is enjoyed by anyone speaking in a court, such as a judge or lawyers, or by MPs in Parliament. Qualified privilege is attached to reports of these proceedings, although there are certain conditions. These conditions are that the report is fair, accurate, without malice and broadcast *contemporaneously* – that is, as soon as possible.

This means that accusations reported may well be malicious and untrue. But, if uttered in an open court or in the Commons and accurately reported as soon as possible, the allegations are protected by privilege and that is an end to the matter.

A defence of qualified privilege is also available to reports of other public proceedings such as council meetings, official tribunals and other meetings to do with matters of public concern. The same defence may be used in relation to a fair and accurate report of a public notice or statement issued officially by the police, a government department or local authority.

Unintentional defamation

Unintentional defamation can result from an innocent confusion of names. It is one reason why the name of a defendant in a court report is rarely enough by itself – an indication of the address, age and perhaps occupation makes confusion with someone else less likely.

Accord and satisfaction

Accord and satisfaction would apply as a libel defence if an apology had already been broadcast and the plaintiff had agreed that it was acceptable redress.

Criminal libel

Criminal libel is a much more serious sort of defamation. This charge can result from obscenity, sedition or blasphemy. A criminal libel action can also stem from a normal civil libel case, if a court decides that the defamation is so serious that it could lead to a breach of the peace.

It is therefore possible to libel criminally a dead person, if a court decides that the surviving relatives were likely to be provoked into a breach of the peace as a result. The penalties for criminal libel include a prison sentence. If there is any suggestion of such a charge, seek legal advice at once.

Contempt

The word contempt in the legal sense might suggest to you something like throwing tomatoes at a judge. While a judge would undoubtedly take a dim view of such conduct and probably impose a severe punishment, the meaning of contempt is rather wider than mere insulting behaviour.

Contempt of court includes any act which is likely to prejudice a forthcoming or current court hearing. In the UK, nobody is allowed to pre-judge a case, to interfere with a trial or influence a jury. There are considerable restrictions on what can be reported while a matter is being considered by a court or *sub judice*. To exceed these defined limits is to risk being in contempt.

To publish the evidence of someone involved in a case after they express it in court is lawful and proper. But to publish the same evidence *in advance* would be contempt. If the witness actively helped with the advance publication, or was paid, the court would take a very serious view and quite possibly jail the witness and those who published his or her words. Someone who also disobeys an order of the court can also be in contempt.

The penalty for contempt is not laid down by law. The theoretical maximum punishment is, therefore, an unlimited fine and a life sentence. In reality, it is not unknown for a contemptuous person to be jailed for an indefinite period. Lawyers say that the jail sentence ends when the guilty person has 'purged his contempt'. This means convincing a judge that he or she is truly sorry and will not repeat the offence. A formal apology in court is often required.

Both criminal and civil cases are both covered by contempt law, but the criminal case is more carefully protected. There are special rules which apply to the reporting of juvenile and matrimonial courts.

In criminal cases, complications can arise if the police are too enthusiastic in saying that they have caught 'the person responsible' for a crime. This is for the court to decide and you should not collude with the police in pre-judging a case.

The key question concerning contempt is whether or not what is broadcast is likely to help or hinder the police in their investigation or undermine the authority of the judicial process.

A *step-by-step guide to contempt*

Contempt is only possible at certain stages in a criminal case. To illustrate this, let us look at the foul and brutal murder of Bill Smith, found battered to death one wet Saturday night outside a pub. This is only intended as a guide. It is your responsibility to make sure you know as much detail as possible about what you can and cannot say.

Stage 1:   *Smith found by police. They appeal for witnesses. Nobody is in custody.*

You can say what you like – as long as it is true, of course. A detective may give an interview describing the 'savage murder' and say he is launching a countywide hunt for a 'dangerous killer who may strike again'.

Stage 2:   *Man arrested. It is the pub landlord. No charge yet.*

You are immediately constrained. Bill Smith has now *not* been murdered. He has 'died'. It is *not* brutal. No adjectives are allowed at all. It is not *the* man who police were seeking who has been arrested but a man. You should not identify the pub landlord, even if an incautious police officer tells you who has been arrested. You could write:

> Detectives in Blanktown have spent the night questioning a man in connection with the death of Bill Smith, whose body was found outside the Red Lion pub in West Street two days ago. Mr Smith, who was 42, lived in Cross Street, Blanktown. Police say they're likely to make a further statement later today.

Stage 3:   *Landlord due in court today, charged with murder*

The word 'murder' may now reappear because you are allowed to say what the charge is. However, other constraints stay. *Think carefully* before naming someone at this stage. What if the charge is withdrawn before the court appearance? The pub landlord could then sue for libel. You can say:

> A man is expected to appear before Blanktown magistrates today charged with the murder of 42-year-old Bill Smith whose body was found outside the Red Lion pub in West Street. Mr Smith lived in nearby Cross Street. His body was discovered by a police officer.

Stage 4:   *Landlord appears in magistrate's court for committal to Crown Court.*

The rules change again. Generally you can now name him, although you should restrict your report to name, age, address, charge and result:

> A 53-year-old pub landlord from Blanktown has appeared before the town's magistrates charged with murder. George Jones, of the Red Lion in West Street, is accused of murdering Bill Smith of Cross Street in Blanktown. Mr Smith's body was found in West Street last Saturday night. Jones has been remanded in custody for seven days.

Stage 5:   *Case goes to Crown Court.*

You may now report what happens each day in court and quote the judge, witnesses, counsel and the defendant himself. The words must have been said during the trial and must not be paraphrased in the report. They must be attributed and allegations clearly signposted by the use of such phrases as 'Prosecuting counsel alleged that . . .'; 'The judge warned the jury not to . . .'; 'The court was told that . . .'. The name of the court must be included, as well as an indication that the case is proceeding: 'The case continues.' Beware of interruptions from the public gallery. In general, these *must not* be reported in detail as they do not form part of the court proceedings and therefore will not be protected from any libel action.

Stage 6:   Jones found guilty of murder.

For the end of the case itself, the rules are the same as in Stage 5:

> The judge told Jones that this was a savage and unprovoked attack . . . and that a life sentence was inevitable. He also recommended that Jones should serve at least 20 years.

Stage 7:   After the case.

You can almost go back to Stage 1. You can broadcast a detective's opinion that 'Jones is a savage man who must stay behind bars for a long time.' You may interview relatives of the murderer or victim. They may say what they like, including criticism of the sentence. The usual rules of libel still apply. It must not, for example, be alleged that the judge, jury or counsel were dishonest, although a solicitor announcing an appeal can identify the grounds for appeal. Also, Jones must not be accused of other crimes, unless he is facing further charges.

Court reporting

Reporting legal proceedings is a skilled job and entire books have been written on the subject.

In practice, radio journalists seldom spend much time in courts. Smaller stations cannot routinely afford to let their journalists sit in a courtroom press box for maybe hours while a case proceeds. Instead, court copy will be filed by news agencies. Their time is well spent because they can send a report of a single case to a number of different outlets – radio, television and newspapers – and, of course, be paid for each one.

So radio journalists are most likely to deal with court copy written by someone else, filed by phone or fax. Such copy may be reduced to a couple of paragraphs or, if more interesting, written as a voicer.

Only in really major cases will most radio journalists go to court. Even in a big case, though, there is little point in allocating a radio reporter in court throughout the hearing. They cannot record the actual proceedings on tape for broadcast, and any interview with a witness or other person involved while a case is in progress would almost certainly constitute a serious contempt of court. Interviews with people involved in a case may be used after the trial is over, so long as what is said is not libellous.

Basic rules

However the information is obtained, there are some basic rules of court reporting which must be followed scrupulously every time:

1. All court reports must identify accused people beyond reasonable doubt, if they are to be named at all. Therefore, a name is rarely sufficient and the address should be given as well. The address may be abbreviated and a house or flat number is never used. It is usual, though not compulsory, to add an age and occupation.

2. It is illegal to identify certain defendants, such as children appearing in a youth court. A woman alleging rape is also entitled to anonymity (see Reporting Restrictions below).

3. The plea must be made clear. It is particularly important that any plea of not guilty is included in each report, but the actual words need not be used. A phrase such as 'Smith denies the charge . . .' is sufficient.

4. The charge or charges must be reported. In a complicated indictment, some abbreviation is customary in a radio report: 'Smith faces nine charges, including one of robbery, as well as insulting behaviour and breach of the peace.'

5. Allegations reported must have actually been made in court and that fact must be made clear: 'The court was told that Smith had drunk seven pints of lager before the assault took place . . .'; 'The jury heard that Smith had visited the bank at least three times before the robbery...'. Such phrases as 'Prosecuting counsel told the jury . . .' are similarly acceptable.

6. Court reports must be balanced as far as possible. If you quote the prosecution case, you must say what the main line of defence is too (although not necessarily in the same report).

7. You must make it clear if your report comes midway through a case. Such reports customarily end with a phrase such as 'The case continues . . .' or 'The case is proceeding . . .'

8. You must obey any special instruction of the court – for example that the name and address of a witness or defendant shall not be broadcast. It is the responsibility of the news agency to make sure that any such instructions are included in their filed copy. Sometimes special points are included in a separate paragraph headed 'Memo to newsdesk.'

9. Before writing your story for radio, read filed court copy *very* carefully, *all* the way through, and query anything doubtful

immediately with the source. If a mistake is broadcast, it is at least a partial defence to show that you took all reasonable steps to check the accuracy of the copy. However, there is no excuse for *ever* guessing any particulars in a court case. The old maxim applies – *if in doubt, leave out*, even if it means dropping a doubtful story entirely for a bulletin until checks are made.

10. Although the proper place to check agency copy is with the agency, some court clerks are willing to help out by confirming, for example, when a case is likely to resume. Any information you obtain from a clerk, though, is your responsibility.

In summary, court reporting for radio usually means converting the copy of someone else who has been writing primarily for print. If you abridge a court report, make sure you omit nothing which affects the balance by, say, leaving out the defence case. Above all, ensure that your report is accurate, does not libel anyone and does not prejudice a case which is proceeding.

Reporting restrictions

An order not to publish or broadcast is known as a reporting restriction. The restriction may be statutory (as in the case of committal proceedings), or it may be made by a judge in a particular case.

Statutory reporting restrictions, contained in Acts of Parliament, are intended to protect certain people. For example, a woman alleged to be the victim of a rape cannot be named and neither can children. However, a child appearing on a joint charge with an adult before a Crown Court can be named in some circumstances. This is an unusual event, and the wise journalist checks the exact position with the court before going ahead with broadcast.

Judges and magistrates have the power to order special reporting restrictions in appropriate case. For example, a judge may order that the name and address of a witness should be withheld if broadcast would place him or her at risk. It is also possible for an order to be made withholding a defendant's name where publication could reasonably help to identify a child in the case.

If you are involved in re-writing court copy, you must be aware if reporting restrictions apply. If they do, it is good practice to include in your story that 'reporting restrictions were not lifted.'

Other cases

Civil law

Civil law cases include any action between two or more parties which results from a conflict of some kind over rights, money or property. The border between civil and criminal cases is very carefully drawn, but it can be fairly narrow.

For example, to refuse to pay for food in a restaurant is not, in itself, a criminal act, in spite of anything the proprietor may say. If the refusal is caused by the low standards of food and if the complainant willingly identifies himself before leaving, it is up to the restaurant owner to sue for his money through the court. If, however, someone tries to leave surreptitiously without paying the bill, or orders food without the means to pay, that is a crime.

Common examples of civil cases include attempts to recover unpaid bills, the allocation of children's custody rights in divorce, and actions for defamation.

Civil cases are heard in the County Court or High Court whereas criminal proceedings begin in a Magistrates' Court (in England and Wales) and proceed to Crown Court if the charge is serious enough. Criminal charges are generally brought by the Crown Prosecution Service following police action, but many civil cases involve arguments between two members of the public only.

A judge in a civil case may make an order in favour of the plaintiff or the defendant at the end of the hearing, and perhaps grant an injunction. This frequently prevents someone acting in a certain way and can be granted temporarily until a case can be fully aired in court. For example, a noisy family might be the subject of an injunction granted to neighbours forbidding them to have parties late at night. If the parties continue, those responsible are in contempt of court and may be punished.

Reporting a civil case involves much the same responsibility as a criminal trial. Reports of what is said in court must be accurate. It is more difficult to be in contempt of a civil case by discussing it in advance, but take care. Before a civil case, you may outline the cause of the argument, but avoid a lot of detail and make sure that a summary of the disagreement is fairly presented. Steer clear of interviews with potential witnesses.

Inquests

An inquest is run by a coroner who is frequently medically qualified. His or her job is to discover the cause of death where it may have been caused by accident or violence. Some serious cases – usually industrial accidents – may include a jury. A coroner sitting alone *records* a verdict. A coroner's jury *returns* a verdict. There are several verdicts which may be reached. They include death by accident, misadventure, justifiable homicide, unlawful killing and suicide. If the cause cannot be established, the result is an 'open' verdict.

Inquests cannot be prejudiced and there is no contempt in this sense. This is because an inquest is not trying to attach any blame to an individual. Beware, though, when reporting suspected suicides. If a woman is found dead in her car with the engine running and a hosepipe from the exhaust fed through a window, you *must not* say it is suicide. That is for the coroner to decide. You can describe the circumstances in which the body was found and use phrases like; 'Police do not suspect foul play...'; 'Detectives say there are no suspicious circumstances . . .'; 'Police aren't looking for anyone in connection with the incident . . .'; If it appears someone has shot himself, all you can say is that the body was found '. . . with a shotgun lying nearby'.

Official secrets

The issue of official secrets is very complex, but few radio journalists will come into conflict with it often. Journalists do not sign the Official Secrets Act but can be prosecuted for publishing information which might be useful to an enemy of state.

The most usual contact between journalists and state secrets is the 'D Notice' (with D standing for Defence). This is a voluntary system which identifies sensitive subjects. It is set up by editors and government officials and overseen by a committee. The publication of a D Notice itself is restricted because they are confidential. Examples of the kind of subjects which could be covered are the locations of military sites, details of equipment on them, details of factories or products involved in defence, and the identities of certain Crown servants. Contravention of a D Notice is not an offence in itself, but might well lead to further action.

12

Newsroom management

Resources

The problem of running any newsroom is that it is expensive. As far as many senior managers in commercial radio are concerned, it is seen as an expensive necessity. They have to balance the need to provide a news service to their listeners (and also that their radio station's Promise of Performance may require it) with the fact that news spends money but rarely brings it in. For the BBC, though, news on local radio is seen as the station's lifeblood and better resources are provided because the news and speech output is greater than that of commercial radio.

Rotas

In a simple news operation, working rotas are easy to put together. The bigger the news operation, the harder rotas become. Do not forget to allow everyone the opportunity for variety within their jobs. Also allow for holidays and days off in lieu when people work weekends. Try to keep people on the same shift throughout the week. It is dispiriting to have to work an 'early' for two days to be followed by the rest of the week on a 'late'. Be aware of individual preferences, but in the end you have the final say and make the decisions (Figure 12.1).

Budgets

As a News Editor, you will be given a working budget. You are responsible for estimating your own costs. If you agree the budget, it is

MAR 11TH – 17TH		Monday 11th	Tuesday 12th	Wednesday 13th	Thursday 14th	Friday 15th	Saturday 16th	Sunday 17th
Network Support Unit:	News							
	News							
	Sport							
Dunstable:								
5-1		Geoff Mike	Geoff Mike	Geoff	Geoff Mike	Geoff Mike	Mike	
10-6		Bill	Bill	Bill	Bill	Bill	Sheila	Doug
		Sheila	Sheila	Sheila	Sheila	Sheila		
Bedford:								
5-1		Ron	Ron	Ron	Ron	Ron		
10-6		Tim	Tim	Tim	Tim	Tim		
Cambridge: 10-6		Kate	Kate	Kate	Kate	Kate		
Northampton: 10-6		Nick	Nick	Nick	Nick	Nick		
5-1		Dave	Dave	Dave	Dave	Dave		
11-7		Cathy	Cathy	Cathy	Cathy	Cathy		
Milton Keynes:								
5-1		Rich	Rich	Rich	Rich	Rich		
10-6		Gemma	Gemma	Gemma	Gemma	Gemma		

Figure 12.1 A newsroom rota for several sites

vital to work within it. The budget you negotiate with your station's senior management will probably be an annual figure. Break this down into a monthly sum and divide it up among all the key areas of expenditure. Keep a careful record of all expenditure, especially invoices for freelance contributions. Suitable headings for budget expenditure include: salaries, freelance cover, agency copy, staff expenses, travel, entertainment, telephones and stationery (Figure 12.2).

Estimating costs

Always try to work out your estimated budget for the year ahead based upon your actual expenditure last year. Study the figures carefully to see where you have overspent and underspent and adjust your estimates accordingly. Be realistic. In a situation where you have to barter for your budget (almost always) with other departments, make sure you are fully prepared to justify your planned expenditure. Allow for inflation and give yourself the flexibility to act within budget. If anything, over-estimate. Think ahead and plan a contingency budget for coverage of unexpected events which may be costly, such as elections.

Cutting costs

You may be required to cut costs for a variety of reasons. For example, it may be because you have overspent your originally agreed budget or that the commercial environment means that cuts are required by all departments of the radio station.

Do not panic. First, try to limit any damage by making sure there is no unnecessary expenditure on copy from agencies or that reporters are incurring unnecessary mileage. If the situation becomes really bad, you will have to consider cutting costs drastically. However, your primary concern must be to protect the output of your newsroom as far as possible. Your aim must be to see through the crisis while creating the cosmetic impression on the air that the service is normal. This means that bulletins should continue unchanged as far as possible.

Here are some suggestions for gradual cost cutting:

• Cut freelance agency copy, especially the coverage of those court cases which are less important.
• Cut all mileage for face-to-face interviews. Only go out on stories

Radio Local News – 1995/6 Budget Submission*

1. News Agency Copy (monthly)

Miles News Agency	30 stories @ £6.36	£190.80
Wheeler's Press Agency	15 stories @ £6.36	£95.40
Ward News Agency	20 stories @ £6.36	£127.20
Abbott's Agency (court copy)	Fixed fee	£180.00
	Monthly Agency Total	£593.40

2. Freelance Journalist Cover (monthly)

Weekend Cover: 8 weekend (Sat/Sun) shifts (or
replacement for staffer) @ £60 per day   £480.00
Holiday cover: 12 staff x 4 weeks' annual leave = 48
weeks to cover. 4 weeks per month @ £300 per week
(£60 per day)   £1200
                                                           Monthly Freelance Total   £1680.00

3. Expenses (monthly)

4 reporters out on road 5 days a week. Average
10 miles a day @ 30p per mile = £15 a week each.

Therefore £60 x 4 weeks		£240.00
Parking and miscellaneous		£50.00
	Monthly Expenses Total	£290.00

4. Sundries (monthly)

Public Relations/Entertainment		£30.00
Training		£50.00
Contingency (Elections, Major Incidents)		£250.00
	Monthly Sundries Total	£330.00

TOTAL MONTHLY NEWSROOM BUDGET (excluding salaries)

	News Agency Cover	£593.40
	Freelance Cover	£1680.00
	Expenses	£290.00
	Sundries	£330.00
	Total Monthly	£2893.40

ANNUAL NEWSROOM RUNNING COSTS

                                   £2893.40 X 12   =   £34,720.80

* This budget excludes salaries and assumes that allowances for telephones, tapes, newspapers,
National Insurance, stationery, depreciation, etc., are allocated to central departments.

Figure 12.2 A typical budget submission

when there is the chance of good audio and background sound. Do not just go to do an interview 'in a quiet corner somewhere'. Do phone interviews, or better still, persuade more interviewees to visit the studio.

- Do not use freelance journalists at all. Cover the shifts with staff.
- Reduce the use of unnecessary stationery. Do not buy extravagant items like high quality pens.
- Reduce the use of the phone. Obviously important check calls need to be done but it is surprising how many unnecessary calls are made. This can be changed with just a little thought before picking up the phone.

If more cuts are needed, you will need to agree with your Programme Director or Managing Editor a re-structuring of the day's news bulletins to ensure that the most effort goes into the bulletins with the biggest audiences, that is (usually) the ones broadcast at breakfast time. Above all, try and make all the cuts without having to make the biggest cut of all – that of making one or more of your staff redundant. People are your greatest resource of all and, as a manager, you should do everything to protect them.

Complaints

No matter how careful you are, mistakes sometimes get through on the air. Most of us do not like saying we are wrong, let alone admitting it publicly by broadcasting a correction. Complaints need to be dealt with and treated seriously.

Phoned complaints

People who phone the newsroom to complain about a story can either be polite or abusive. Whatever their attitude, you should remain calm and courteous. First ask for a name, address and telephone number. If they have a genuine complaint, they will not object. If the complaint is unjustified or on a minor matter, this will discourage them. Then let the person explain fully why they are upset. Try not to interrupt or go on the defensive. Take notes. Sometimes the very act of being able to talk to someone about the complaint will enable them to 'get it off their chest' and they will not want to take matters further. Whatever happens, *act* rather than *react*. The best advice is to say you will look into the matter and call them back. Most stations require a log to be kept of all complaints and some provide a form to be filled in.

Correcting errors

Check that a mistake really has been made. There are a surprising number of complaints made to broadcasters on the basis of something which has been mis-heard or heard on another radio station with a similar name. Some complainants have even been told about something by a third party who has relayed an incorrect account of what was actually broadcast. Check the computer archive file, the clip-up file or the logger tape (a slow-speed recording which has been made of the station's output which is kept for a period of time).

If you are at fault, ring back and try to smooth ruffled feelings by apologising. Never put the blame somewhere else. If the inaccurate report came from a freelance agency, you simply say the report came from an experienced journalist and was broadcast in good faith. It is difficult to decide on action other saying sorry privately. Sometimes, a listener will demand an on-air apology. If you are wrong, you should say so but on-air apologies will be rare and sanctioned only by a senior member of staff. They should be broadcast in a timeslot corresponding to when the story was first aired.

Remember that listeners will in general have greater respect for you if you admit your mistakes and do not try to hide them.

Solicitors

A solicitor's letter can be daunting when received in a newsroom. Do not panic if you receive one. However, never ignore it (Figure 12.3).

Usually it will request a transcript of the broadcast. It is up to you whether or not you supply this transcript. In the end you can be forced to do so. The best advice when dealing with solicitors is to use your own legal advisers. Although this is expensive, it is nevertheless important to make sure your legal dealings are correct and everything is done properly. Your solicitor will advise you on what to admit, if anything, and also draft any reply.

In the unlikely event of you having to reply to a solicitor's letter on your own, be sure to include the words 'without prejudice'. This means

CHANTLER, HARRIS & CO.
SOLICITORS AND COMMISSIONERS FOR OATHS

BANK CHAMBERS, 14 TAVISTOCK STREET
CANNING, SOMERSET CG1 4ER
TELEPHONE CANNING 23908 (5 LINES)
FACSIMILE CANNING 33618

The News Editor
Newtoon Radio Limited
Tolworth Cross
Canning
CG2 4RR

14th June 1996
Our ref.   MBW/AG

Dear Sir

re Newtoon Radio News, 1st June 1996

We are instructed by Mr. John Doe, Managing Director of AB Engineering Limited, Priorswood, Canning, concerning an interview broadcast on the above programme with Mr. Richard Roe, Chief Shop Steward of the Associated Operators Union.

You are of course aware that there is currently a dispute between our client's Employer Company and the Associated Operators Union. We are instructed that the following words of Mr Roe, quoted verbatim, were broadcast by yourselves: "The real problem is that the management of ABE are incompetent. I don't think the Managing Director could measure a piece of string and get the right answer. They can't manage anything, and they don't know much about engineering either, for what I can see."

Your legal advisors must surely have informed you that the dissemination of such a statement by Wessex Radio is defamatory of our client and we are instructed to seek damages in libel from yourself for its broadcast.

Since it took place our client has found difficulty in the business community in handling the affairs of the company due to the wholly unjustified attack of Mr. Roe broadcast by yourselves.

We enclose a form of apology which we require to be broadcast on the same programme within seven days of today at a point in the programme commensurately prominent to the original broadcast. Please advise us by return when the broadcast will take place.

Furthermore, unless we receive written confirmation within seven days of your preparedness to pay a reasonable sum in damages for your libel against our client, a writ seeking damages, together with a claim for interest and costs, will be issued without further reference to yourselves.

We look forward to hearing from you within the time limit specified.

Yours faithfully

A

for Chantler, Harris & Co.

GEORGE BURROWS, STEPHEN BURROWS, MICHAEL WOOLACOTT LL.B., JULIAN RUNDLE

THIS FIRM IS REGULATED BY THE LAW SOCIETY FOR INVESTMENT BUSINESS

Figure 12.3 A (fictitious) solicitor's letter alleging libel. Make sure you always use your solicitors to reply

your letter is legally off-the-record. Make sure your company is covered by specific insurance which is available to broadcasters in case you are taken to court for libel.

In the BBC, you have access to 24-hour-a-day legal advice through the corporation's lawyers. A check with the duty solicitor is, of course, free to BBC journalists.

Regulatory authorities

The three main regulatory authorities you may have dealings with are the Radio Authority (in commercial radio), the Broadcasting Complaints Commission and the Broadcasting Standards Council.

The Radio Authority is responsible for the regulation of its commercial licensees' programming, advertising and transmissions. The Authority requires stations to keep recordings of all broadcasts for 42 days. Outside this time, there may be no recordings to which to refer and complaints may not be pursued. It will investigate complaints of inaccuracy, bias and offensiveness, taking action if necessary. It can admonish the company, request a broadcast apology or correction, and also impose a penalty which can include a fine and even the shortening or revocation of a licence. The Authority publishes a number of Codes of Practice including one for news and current affairs.

The Broadcasting Complaints Commission is a statutory body and deals with complaints from those who feel they have been unfairly treated or had their privacy invaded. After adjudication on a complaint about a station, the Commission may require broadcast of its findings.

The Broadcasting Standards Council considers complaints about violence, sexual conduct and taste and decency in programmes and advertisements. Again, after adjudication, the Council may require broadcast of its findings.

From April 1997, the BCC and BSC will become one body called the Broadcasting Standards Commission.

Privacy

Many complaints to newsrooms centre around an alleged invasion of privacy. You should remember the following:

Phone interviews are potentially dangerous. Anyone who is recorded in a phone interview must be told that he or she is talking to a radio station and must give his or her consent to the interview being broadcast.

Hidden microphones should only be used as a last resort. Before broadcasting anything recorded with a hidden microphone, advice needs to be sought from senior management in the BBC or the Radio Authority for commercial radio.

Intercepted radio. It is illegal to rebroadcast any material recorded off air from the emergency services or aircraft.

Children. Any interviewing of children without parental permission requires great care. They should not be interviewed about private family matters.

Winning audiences

News has to be seen in the context of the programming of the radio station as a whole. There is no point in broadcasting news if nobody is listening. With most radio sets now equipped with push-button pre-set tuning, it is all too easy for a listener to switch to another station if something is broadcast which bores or irritates or is irrelevant. It is therefore the job of the newsroom as well as other programmers to contribute to the overall of aims of the radio station of keeping as many people listening for as long as possible.

Audience figures

The success of a station is usually judged on audience figures. These are the key to earning revenue for commercial stations and for justifying the licence fee within the BBC.

Audience figures for both the BBC and commercial radio are produced by RAJAR (Radio Audience Joint Research) which is the company set up to manage the UK's agreed system of audience measurement. Diaries are placed in a demographically-selected and representative number of households in a specific area and people are asked to keep a record of their radio listening, not only to which station but also for how long. This data is then analysed and audience figures are produced.

The RAJAR surveys – or 'sweeps' – take place continuously. However, most local stations have results only once or twice a year, depending on the size of the potential audience. The sweep is for a period of three months and the figures are then analysed and published six weeks or so later.

The figures show the weekly 'reach' of a station – that is the number of listeners who tune in for a set minimum period over a week – expressed in thousands of listeners or a percentage of the total population. They also show 'average hours' – that is the average number of hours a listener tunes in each week – and also the 'market share' or percentage of total radio listening enjoyed by a station compared to others in the area. It is possible to see the total number of people listening every half hour to the radio station throughout the day and analyse their demographic makeup. For example, you can tell whether a station particularly appeals to females aged 25–34 or males aged 55 and over.

Targeting audiences

A growing number of news editors believe that they not only have to consider radio's traditional advantages over other media as a source of news, but take this a step further by targeting stories to specific groups of listeners.

They consider the format of the station when making decisions about the editorial agenda and what stories to cover. For example, a 'hotter hits' pop station needs to have stories about pop personalities in its news to make it relevant and a black music station needs stories about the black community. It is your job to tell your listener what is going on with specific reference to his or her interests. One way their interest can be identified is the fact they are tuned to your station and therefore enjoy the music it plays. Use this as a cue to target stories about that music and related affairs. If your audience is in the 25–44 age group, it is important to highlight stories about home-buying and bringing up children. If your audience is 55+, you might need to be talking more about retirement issues.

Take careful note of the audience figures and the demographic breakdown of the listenership. This will give you a clue as to your editorial agenda. The key advice when targeting audience is to make your stories *relevant*.

Many stations are now including news and an audience's news values in specially-commissioned audience research projects such as focus group discussions where listeners described their likes and dislikes in news. Beware, though, that listeners speaking in groups often say what they think you want to hear rather than what they actually think. Such research should be used simply as a tool and just one of the things a news editor or programme director makes use of to improve output.

You should never be led blindly by research alone.

Presentation formats

There are a variety of different ways of presenting news on the radio. The most traditional is the top-of-the-hour news bulletins. Some stations, though, prefer news at five minutes to the hour, half past or even 20 past. Their reasoning is that their rivals in a crowded marketplace carry news at the top of the hour and if they are playing music then, they have a chance to picking up any listeners who may tune out because of a news bulletin.

Rolling news is another format. This means there are constant news updates throughout the clock hour, either read by the presenter or newsreader. BBC local radio is now required to be mostly speech in output and many stations are totally speech at peak times. This speech will include not only extended news bulletins but also live interviews and topical features.

Other formats which are becoming more popular include the 'double header', with a DJ and a newsreader co-presenting a show which takes in music as well as an informal, chatty look at the news. Live interviews can also be incorporated into this format. Another sort of double header is becoming popular on commercial stations where the news presenter is part of a breakfast show 'crew' or 'posse' consisting of the DJ, travel reporter and other studio personnel. It is important where this happens to ensure that, among all the fun and frivolity, the news presenter does not become too embroiled in the entertainment that he or she loses the credibility with which to present serious, often tragic, news stories.

Make the style and sound of your news bulletins or programmes match the radio station style as a whole. It is no use having BBC World Service style presentation on a Top 40 music station or vice versa. Think of the listener and what is relevant. Whatever style of presentation you choose, the important thing is to make sure your bulletins are authoritative and believable.

Promos

Remember the value of good promotion of news. Tell people how good your news bulletins are. Other aspects of the radio station are 'sold' on the air, why not your news? If something is worth doing well, it is worth promoting well.

Sponsorship?

Sponsorship of news bulletins is not allowed in UK commercial radio. This is because of fear that editorial independence could be compromised. For example, if your sponsor was a chemicals company, it could be difficult to do a story criticising that firm.

However, news is an expensive business and there are arguments to say that it would help if news was sponsored just like other parts of the station's output such as the travel and weather news. There is no shortage of companies willing to have their name associated with a news bulletin because of the authority it conveys. Many commercial stations carry special advertisements called Newslink at peak times. These are commercials juxtaposed to the news bulletin and therefore command a premium price. IRN finances the cost of its operation by the sale of these commercials and even gives a proportion of the revenue back to the stations which have 'bartered' their airtime. In this way, stations do not pay a fee for the IRN service and indeed earn money from it.

Perhaps in the future more direct sponsorship of news bulletins will be allowed, easing the burden of financing news gathering for small stations. However, if this happens, it will be vitally important to maintain the editorial integrity of the news and ensure there are guarantees of editorial independence. Existing advertisers are unable to influence a story which criticises them or brings them bad publicity and future sponsors must agree to similar controls.

13

Small newsrooms

Many smaller radio stations are coming on the air. Although these stations have small budgets, it is still possible to set up an effective newsroom with just one or two journalists. However, the skills and organisation needed are different from the way in which larger newsrooms operate. The key thing to remember is that you cannot do everything, certainly not at once. Do not try. Learn to create priorities and deal with them in order (Figure 13.1).

1. Create your own space
2. Acquire personal computer, chair, desk, telephone, headed notepaper, and A–Z book for contacts, large size diary, filing cabinet
3. Acquire portable tape recorder, microphone, dubbing facilities from cassette to cart, open-reel tape recorder, facilities for recording telephone calls, carts, labels, editing kit
4. Contact emergency services
5. Contact MPs and councils
6. Contact voluntary organisations
7. Contact freelance journalists
8. Create filing system to cope with flow of information
9. Create a calls list
10. Agree times of news bulletins with Programme Director
11. Recruit staff if budget allows
12. Start making a list of potential stories
13. Start getting interviews 'in the can' for the first few days of broadcasting
14. Look for an exclusive or two for the first day's broadcasting
15. Start dummy-running news bulletins using your calls list and writing from press releases and conducting follow-up interviews

Figure 13.1 Checklist for setting up a small newsroom

Setting up

First tasks

When you are given the job of setting up a small newsroom, you will usually find that the radio station is far from ready. Building work will be going on all around you and you will be lucky if you even have access to a phone.

You first need to create your own space – one room preferably – with a phone, desk, chair, word processor and printer, a supply of headed notepaper, an A–Z book for contacts, a desk diary and a filing cabinet. Of course, this needs to be complemented eventually by the necessary broadcast equipment to get on the air. Once you have these basic requirements, you can start the main job of talking to people and getting a flow of news coming into the radio station. Ideally you need at least three weeks for this, although it has been done in less time.

Making contacts

Your main task, after setting up your basic newsroom, must be to let people know who you are, when you will be broadcasting and how to get in touch with you.

In the first instance, you should target the emergency services (police, fire, ambulance and, if appropriate, coastguard), the councils and local MPs. Your next priority after that is to contact as many voluntary organisations as possible. You will also need to acquaint yourself with local freelance journalists and news agencies.

It is usually worth phoning the emergency services' press officers and then arrange to visit them. You should have a list of all your phone numbers and take some radio station publicity material with you. Try and make friends with them. Bear in mind they will have other priorities as far as the press and broadcasters are concerned and you will be an unknown quantity. Tell them about your station, its target audience, on-air date, its news output and what you need from them. It is important to agree a set of times you can do check calls with them.

You need also to visit the press offices of the local district and county councils. Arrange for your address to be added to their mailing lists so you can receive council papers, agenda, minutes and press releases. Ask if you write a letter to all their members. Do this, photocopy it and ask if the council could include it in their next mailout. It needs to tell people you exist and how to get in contact with you.

Also write to the MPs with the same information. Make contact with the local voluntary organisations. Usually there is an 'umbrella' organisation to which all voluntary groups in an area belong. Ask them if you can write a circular letter to their member groups which they can distribute in their next mailshot. Go through the same process with organisations such as the local Chamber of Trade.

All the time you need to be selling your station, its potential audience and yourself. You need to be promoting the ways in which radio in general, and your station in particular, can help them. Very soon you will have an impressive flow of news material coming into your new newsroom.

Technical requirements

The minimum you need is a portable audio recorder and microphone, facilities for dubbing from cassette onto cartridge or computer hard disk, facilities for recording phone interviews, editing facilities either on open reel tape or on computer screen, a studio where you can record face-to-face interviews, and a good supply of cassettes, carts, tape, labels and editing kit.

Filing systems

With the amount of press releases and council papers flowing into the newsroom, you will need to set up a proper filing system to cope with it all. You need to create the following files:

Diary file – Two sets of files labelled 1 to 31, corresponding to the days of the month. Use one set for this month, the other for next month. Set aside a special file for beyond that. As events come into the newsroom, enter them under the appropriate date in the desk diary and file the relevant paperwork under the date in your file.

Contacts file – Some newsrooms prefer to list the names of contacts in a book with an A–Z index. You can also set up an on-screen contacts file on your computer system.

Background file – File background information, newspaper cuttings, press releases and so on under the appropriate heading. Have a file for each council and emergency service, as well as files on such subjects as schools, buses, trains and specific running stories.

Archive file – Once you are on the air, you need to file all your bulletin and voicer scripts for reference purposes. There are a number of ways of doing this. In a computerised newsroom, you can set up such files on your system. One of the easiest systems in a newsroom working off paper is to have a ring binder file for each month and file the copy there after each day's broadcasting.

Letters file – Keep a copy of each letter you receive as well as any you send. Subject headings help.

Futures file – Maintain a general file of potential or forthcoming stories, culled from newspaper clippings or press releases.

There is also one more file – arguably the most important of all. It is the 'circular' file – the dustbin. In the early days of a newsroom, it is important to keep as much as possible because you never know what may be useful, but you will start to receive unsolicited commercial junk releases which have no relevance to your audience at all. Throw them away. But be careful to read *everything* you receive. You never know where a good story may be lurking!

Calls list

Your list of calls to the emergency services either needs writing down on paper, displaying on a large easy-to-read board or, preferably, stored in the memory buttons of your phone system. It needs to have all the phone numbers you use regularly and, if the list is written, the rank of officer you need to ask for when you get through. Direct lines should be used where possible, especially for the voice-bank recorded information.

When setting up the list and going to see the emergency services, try to agree a set of regular times when you can include them in a 'round of calls'. For example, a station broadcasting news bulletins from 6am to 3pm daily) needs to make the calls at 5am, 9am, 12 noon and 5pm. The important thing is to make sure the frequency of your calls is sufficient to satisfy your editorial needs without making yourself too much of a nuisance.

Going on air

Preparing for the first day

There are innumerable jobs to be done simultaneously in readiness for the first day the station goes on the air.

Apart from making contacts and creating files, you should start looking for potential stories and getting interviews 'in the can'. Try to assemble a list of potential stories as you make contacts. Ask each contact what he or she sees as the biggest local issue. Read the local newspapers thoroughly. Use the run-up to on-air as the opportunity to gather as much material as possible. Remember, this is a comparative luxury. After the station goes on the air, you will be responsible for putting out daily news bulletins and will just not have the time to rush around everywhere recording interviews and talking to people in depth. Then you will be relying on the quality of the contacts you have built up during this period.

You will also need to be discussing with the programme director the quantity and scheduling of news to be broadcast each day. Should there be a bulletin each hour when the station is staffed by a journalist? Or is that journalist better used by gathering material for the following morning? It is obviously important for the main news bulletins to be scheduled hourly during breakfast time when the biggest potential audience is available. But should you have half-hour headlines or updates every 20 minutes? These are questions which need to be answered in talks with the programmes and balanced against the resources and staff you have available. Try not to do too much too soon. It is easier to build up something than to start with a superb service which you then have to cut because there are insufficient resources.

Getting exclusives

During the run-up to on-air, aim to get a number of 'exclusives' ready for the first few days of broadcasting. Bear in mind that a lot of listeners will be trying the station out on its first few days, so it is important to make as big an impact as possible. Look for new angles on long-running local sagas; persuade a local VIP to comment on something he or she feels strongly about; find out about new developments or plans for the area. The criteria for these exclusives should be to find a story which affects your listeners directly or something about which they will have strong feelings. Remember to keep one exclusive for launch day and two others for subsequent use during the first week.

Recruiting staff

Your station may only have the budget to employ you in the newsroom or you may be lucky enough to have the money to recruit other people. If the latter is the case, it is likely that you will have come to the area experienced in broadcasting but without detailed local knowledge. It is therefore important to recruit someone with that essential local awareness.

The best place to try is the local newspaper. You will probably have contact with these journalists in any case as they will be writing stories about the new radio station for their own papers. Always be on the lookout for the newspaper journalist who has an interest in radio and is looking for a break.

If the budget allows, try advertising in the trade press. Care is needed in wording the advertisement. You need to be specific about duties, responsibilities, opportunities and salary.

Try to compile a shortlist of candidates and invite them for an interview. You should be present, as should the Programme Director. You should look for the following qualities:

- a good voice
- an easygoing and adaptable personality
- evidence of professional skills
- evidence of an interest in radio
- an eye for detail
- training in the basics of law
- knowledge of public administration
- experience of (or at least an interest in) the technicalities of radio
- local knowledge

Overall it is important to recruit the person with whom you feel you can best work. You are going to have to work together as a tight team. You need someone who is dependable and will work hard and whose skills complement your own. They need to have a good deal of common sense and a healthy attitude.

Training and coaching

If they have no experience of radio but you feel they have the right potential, they need to be trained in the rudiments quickly. Ideally, send them for experience at a working station or get them booked on one of the basic skills radio training courses. You could even give them a copy of this book!

Remember that training staff on the job is vital for their career development and so you can delegate more tasks to them. As a News Editor whether in a small or large newsroom, the value of individual coaching is immense; always take the trouble to listen to a tape of a package or news bulletin and let your team member know what you do not like (and, of course, equally important is to let them know what you do like!).

One good idea is a 'copy clinic' where you analyse the good and bad points of a sample of a journalist's cues and scripts.

14

Specialist programmes

The news round-up

The news round-up programme is different from a bulletin in that it may use older stories and also longer versions of stories.

Older stories means by hours, not days. A news programme at, say, 6pm may well include anything from that day's events that is worth having and is still current or can be adapted to be current. Many listeners will have heard nothing since they left for work at 8.15am.

Presentation of these programmes will be different too. For example, they can be double-headed – in other words, using two presenters. The style can be less formal, even chatty, and there may well be 'guest appearances' from other people giving travel and financial reports (Figure 14.1).

A typical format

Here is a fictional, but typical, format for an evening news programme on a commercial station, anchored in 'flip-flop' style by two presenters:

7	00:00	Opening signature tune with headlines – JANE
	00:30	Teasers – JANE
	01:00	News bulletin – JOHN
	05:00	Travel – JUSTINE (via AA Roadwatch)
	06:30	AD BREAK 1
	09:00	Live interview 1 – JANE
	11:00	Package 1 – CUED BY JOHN

Figure 14.1 A talks studio at BBC Ulster, complete with microphones, headphones and portable clock. Also note the cue light on the table – it is more visible in front of the broadcaster than it would be on the wall.
Courtesy: Tim Arnold

13:00	AD BREAK 2
15:00	Headlines – JANE
16:00	Financial report
18:00	Live interview 2 – JOHN
21:00	Sport – MICHAEL
25:00	AD BREAK 3
27:00	Package 2 (1'30") – CUED BY JANE
28:30	Headlines – JOHN (Prefade signature tune at 29:00)
29:20	Closing sequence – JANE and JOHN
29:59	Signature tune out

This type of programme is designed for an evening audience who may well be driving home and dipping in and out every few minutes. You would not have to hear the whole programme to get a reasonable idea of the day's main news stories and you would probably hear at least one in depth.

The note to 'prefade' the one-minute signature tune at 29:00 means that the music will run from 29:00 to 29:59. It can be faded up at any time and still end neatly on schedule. This is the job of the Producer, Technical Operator or Studio Manager.

A programme like this is not generally driven by the presenters because they do not have enough time to check that everything is ready, including the three 'guest' reporters, two live interviews and the commercial breaks, as well as present the programme.

Since this schedule is fairly tight, in reality the second package would probably be an expendable item. One and a half minutes can easily be absorbed by a couple of extra commercials or an overrun by the financial or sports presenter.

Jingles and 'beds'

Jingles and idents (identity music 'stabs') play an important part in keeping a programme like this moving. There will be separate versions of the signature tune for the start and finish and probably several short versions which are recognisably part of the same piece, maybe between three and ten seconds long. These can be played at intervals during the programme, such as around the headline sequence, to maintain continuity and remind the listener what the programme is all about.

Many stations like using music 'beds' over which headlines can be used. Take care to choose music which is non-intrusive and be especially careful with the volume at which the music is played as many listeners, especially those in cars, sometimes find it difficult to hear what is being said over poorly balanced music beds.

Features and documentaries

Feature pieces are a chance to tell a story in more depth. A package or wrap consists of at least one clip of audio, which is linked by a reporter to make a complete story. A package is, in effect, a voicer with some audio inserted into it. A news package may run 35 seconds or so with just one piece of audio; at the other end is the news documentary, which may run for an hour and have dozens of clips in it.

In each case, the basic principles are the same. Audio should add to the story, not just repeat what the reporter has just said. Each link into each clip can be treated like a separate news cue, except that the opening line of each cue does not, of course, start the story from scratch. Each cue should move the overall story on in some way by expanding an earlier part or contradicting it.

The great advantage of a feature is that, by using appropriate audio, both sides of an argument can be aired in the same piece. Often, conflicting views have greater impact if they are heard in quick succession by the listener. Another point to note is that longer features can be far more creative, using sound effects and music as well as speech.

The essence

Here is the beginning of a fictitious documentary about railways:

FX: Bristol Temple Meads station. Atmos at 5am. Down and under...

REPORTER: Temple Meads station, Bristol, at five in the morning. Most of the city is fast asleep ... but Temple Meads never sleeps. Even at Christmas there are still people on duty, even though no trains run for the public. The area manager is Chris Potts...

POTTS: In: 'We can never close a station...

            Out: '...day or night, we are here.'

            Station sounds.

FX: Down and under...

REPORTER: Every day, thousands of people use Temple Meads. To deal with them, there are staff like Leading Railman Lee Kavanagh...

KAVANAGH: In: 'My dad joined the Great Western Railway in...'

The radio documentary must have a shape and a story to tell. You, as producer, must know whether it will have a definite conclusion to reach, or whether it is a series of individual pictures in sound, put together because they are more effective in a single frame. Remember that other people's words are often more effective than your own, and that there are many sounds other than words. This is the essence of documentary making. Use all these resources and your documentary will be memorable.

Setting up

The making of a documentary is hard work. On a local radio station, it may be a single-handed job. If you need to interview perhaps 20 people, that means 20 separate appointments to be made and kept. Try not to get too much audio from each one. If you record half hour interviews, that adds up to ten hours of continuous speech to assess later! Editing on this timescale can be tremendously time-consuming. So rationalise your efforts at the start. If you will want at the most one minute from each person in the finished production, ten interview minutes recorded should be enough unless the interviewee turns out to be particularly fascinating.

Make sure that you have access to the music and sound effects you need. Is your documentary one of a series? If so, does the series have a distinctive house style – a standard beginning and end with its own signature tune? Any standard introduction will have to be accommodated in your particular piece.

Editing

Be ruthless when you edit a documentary. It is a common mistake to include too much. A one-hour documentary on a commercial station is actually 48 minutes; the other 12 minutes are taken up by commercial breaks and the hourly news. In those 48 minutes, you will do well to include more than about 35 minutes of audio, unless your own contributions are very brief.

Look for voices and sounds that are startling and consider one to end your documentary. Go out on a bang, if that is appropriate to your subject. Make the listener listen by the force of your material and do not let it sag. If something seems rather boring, leave it out. Keep the pace moving and use shorter rather than longer clips of audio.

Finally, a complete programme must be recorded in good time before transmission. Do not forget to book a studio and anyone needed to drive the audio inserts while you record the links between each one. Or you can self-op as you would a bulletin. If possible, allow some time between the master recording and the transmission date. Editing documentaries on the day of transmission is not unknown, but work done in a hurry may not be your best.

Outside broadcasts

Planning an outside broadcast – or OB for short – is like planning a battle. You must have everyone in the correct place at the correct time with the correct equipment (Figure 14.2).

Many of the difficulties encountered on outside broadcasts are technical rather than personal. The hospital to be visited by royalty next week will turn out to be in a low part of the area where radio links are not effective. This means either an ISDN landline or driving to nearby high ground with freshly recorded material and transmitting it from there.

Generally, outside broadcasts must be planned ahead as far as possible – preferably at least one month before. For example, deciding to cover a royal visit the day before will be pointless – in practice, a reporter is unlikely to be allowed anywhere near without the precious 'Royal Rota' pass issued to journalists by the Central Office of Information. You must apply for these passes well in advance.

Figure 14.2 The showbiz side of outside broadcasts. Pop group Code Red perform live on the Essex FM '2 Smart 4 Drugs' schools roadshow in association with Essex Police and Essex Drug Action Team

There are a number of ways of getting material back from an outside broadcast and each has its own set of advantages and problems. The main ways are:

- radio links
- ISDN landlines
- telephone links
- courier

Radio links

The UHF radio link is one of the most common ways of doing outside broadcasts in local radio. The transmitter in the station radio car or radio van uses an ultra high frequency that is well outside that available on domestic radio receivers, but it can be heard by anyone with the right equipment; it is not, therefore, watertight. Anything sent back to the studio in this way is therefore being broadcast. Such a link is also vulnerable to the failures of aerials or transmitters. It may well be useless in some kinds of situations, such as low ground or areas well screened by trees or tall buildings.

If radio links are to be used, a site check in advance is essential. On the day, beware that other electrical equipment could cause interference.

ISDN landlines

An increasingly popular way of sending material back to the studio from an outside broadcast is by the use of temporary ISDN lines (ISDN stands for Integrated Services Digital Network). These are high quality phones capable of sending full quality stereo signals via dial-up lines throughout the world. However, you need to plan ahead as telephone companies take a few days to install the necessary facilities. Many stations are now installing permanent ISDN points at key buildings throughout their area, such as theatres and council offices, to make it easier to link to the studio on a dial-up basis when necessary.

Telephone links

The telephone provides only low quality output, adequate for a reporter's voice but not much else. Mobile phones can be used but sometimes the signal is weak and using them for live work is usually a last resort. If you have to use a phone to go on the air, try and use a landline phone.

Couriers

Using a motorcycle courier to bring recordings back to the studio means that all semblance of live outside broadcasting is lost. There is no chance of reacting to sudden events at the OB site. Coverage restricted to a courier service is not really an outside broadcast at all.

Standby presenters

Outside broadcasts are still risky in terms of being confident that everything will be working properly as planned. They need to be carefully thought out, well ahead. It is likely that at least two of the communication methods outlined here will have some role. One more element is also crucial for OBs – the availability of a standby presenter in the studio to cover emergency breakdowns.

Phone-ins

For many years, the phone-in programme has been the staple diet of local radio. Critics say it is no more than a cheap way of filling airtime, but properly produced phone-ins can be provocative, interesting and useful. What determines the success of a phone-in is the way it is put together and planned.

Selecting subjects

There are a number of different sorts of phone-in which include:

- an 'open line' discussion on current affairs in general

Figure 14.3
Presenter Dave Monk hosting the morning phone-in at BBC Essex. Note how Dave wears his headphones so that he can hear not only the output but also the resonance of his own voice. Also note how the faders in the BBC are pulled towards you to open them. In commercial radio, they are pushed up

Figure 14.4 Studio assistant Yvette Lee lining up phone-in calls and using the inter-studio visual talkback unit at BBC Essex

- an advice line with a guest such as a doctor or lawyer
- a topical discussion on one particular subject with a guest such as an MP or celebrity

When planning an open line programme or topical general discussion, the best source of material is undoubtedly daily newspapers, local and national. These often provide the spur to which the listener can relate.

Studio operations

It is possible for the presenter to take calls off air and then 'line them up' while a record is playing, if the phone-in consists of music as well as calls. However, the best way of running a phone-in is to have calls 'screened' or answered by an assistant (Figures 14.3 and 14.4).

The assistant needs to note the caller's name, the area from where they are calling and a phone number (for reference). The caller is then put on hold and the details passed to the presenter, either on paper or by means of a visual talkback unit, such as a computer screen onto which words are typed in the control room and appear simultaneously in the studio.

Before the caller goes on the air, he or she needs to be told to turn their radio volume down to avoid 'howl round' or feedback or indeed the effects of an electronic delay system (see below). The programme assistant also needs to make sure the caller is sensible, with a legitimate question or point of view.

Another way of running a phone-in is to invite calls before the programme starts, take callers' phone numbers and call them back while on the air. This gives you much more control over the editorial direction and development of the programme.

Phone-in presenters

Phone-in presenters need to be fluent, witty, wise, provocative and occasionally rude. They need to be positive and stimulate conversation. This often means assuming a point of view and playing devil's advocate. It goes without saying they need to be quick-thinking, alert to defamatory or contemptuous comments from callers and sufficiently broad minded and democratic to let all callers put their points.

The delay

Some stations insist on an electronic delay system to regulate phone-ins. This means that the whole programme is shifted in time for about ten seconds via either a special tape machine or similar digital device. The reason is that if a caller says something defamatory or obscene, this can be deleted a few seconds before transmission and the delayed recording can be replaced by a jingle to avoid the offending remark going out.

Problem phone-ins

You need enormous sensitivity to handle a problem phone-in, which have been accused of being exploitative and the aural equivalent of voyeurism. It is a great responsibility and has to be taken seriously.

Expert guests are needed, such as psychiatrists, doctors and lawyers to handle the calls about sexual and relationship issues, medical conditions and legal queries. Remember, the callers are using the radio station as a friend who can give specialist, unbiased personal advice. During this type of phone-in, you are no longer 'broadcasting' but 'narrowcasting' and talking to the individual, hoping that other listeners – who might never be courageous enough to phone – can identify with the particular problem being discussed.

The music-speech mix

The local radio programme which mixes both speech and music is probably one of the most difficult to do well. It is the ultimate test of the all-round broadcaster, combining the music skills of the DJ with the skills of a reporter. It is hard and demanding work but can be highly satisfying and rewarding.

Qualities of presenter

The presenter needs to be at home handling music, interviews, scripts and studio equipment. In addition, a logical, well-organised mind is required with the ability to think quickly and react to what is

Figure 14.5 Essex FM breakfast show DJ Martin Day stands to present his zany show

happening. A good working knowledge of current affairs and the ability to ad lib rather than simply relying on scripts is an asset, as is the ability to talk 'to time'. In short, you need to be able to cope with anything and everything. In general, it is easier for a journalist to adapt to becoming a music presenter than the other way round.

The right mix

In most programmes, it is necessary to make sure there is not too much speech or too much music. The exact proportion will be defined by the station policy; for example, BBC local radio stations have a policy of no less than 80% speech at peak listening times.

Arguably the safest rule for mixing music and speech is to limit speech items to no more than four minutes, the average length of a song. This means listeners are likely to stay tuned through something in which they are not interested simply because they know it will not last long and something more appealing may follow. An interview with a celebrity, for example, could be spread out in three four-minute segments with music in between, rather than in one 12-minute block.

Music selection is particularly important in programmes which have a speech content. All the music must be familiar and popular in order to prevent the listener tuning out simply because they do not recognise something. Listeners are remarkably tolerant of music they do not like which has been a hit just because it is familiar to them. The idea is to keep the listener listening for as long as possible. You need constantly to tease what is coming up in the programme, including features, interviews and music.

Blending

The programme is likely to consist of audio, packages, live phone interviews, studio guests, links to the radio car, links to unattended studios, a phone-in element, traffic and travel news, sports news and, of course, music. It requires the highest standards of professionalism to blend all these things together slickly.

The key to all this preparation is being well organised in advance. Before going on air, everything needs to be sorted so you know exactly what you are going to use and when you are going to use it. Interview introductions need to have been scripted and a few questions prepared in advance in case there is a distracting panic to do with some other part of the programme just before the live interview.

When you are on the air, you need to be thinking about five or ten minutes ahead of yourself to ensure that the next item is all ready to go. You should always have a music CD cued up in case of emergencies.

If you are creating a new programme, the best advice is not to be too ambitious at first. Start small and build up the content gradually as you become more adept at handling the technical and editorial complexity of the programme.

Try to develop the skill of voicing over the introductions of songs (Figure 14.5). It is, of course, important you do not talk over the vocals. Most DJs find they can do this after a while through instinct, although you might need to watch the CD timer at first. The effect of this is that voicing over intros helps to blur the edges between the music and speech and prevent the 'stop–start' type of presentation which sounds dated.

Elections

Elections make good radio. There is the buzz of the count, the excited claims of rival candidates and the dramatic moment when the result is revealed.

However, the law takes a stern view of anyone who prejudices the fairness of an election. You must be sure that your radio station does not let enthusiasm overtake prudence and that you follow the rules. There is a timetable which lays down what may and must not be done according to the Representation of the People Act 1983 ('the RPA'). As soon as an election is announced, this timetable takes shape. We will deal here with General Elections, although the rules for media coverage of local elections are similar (Figure 14.6).

Election pending

From the moment when the election is announced, Parliament is dissolved and, until nominations close, you would be wise to steer clear of all potential candidates. The election is now pending. At a local government election, the pending period usually begins five weeks before election day.

Closing of nominations

This is the first important stage when all would-be candidates must make sure they have been validly nominated. At this stage, all 'prospective parliamentary candidates' cease to be prospective. From now on, you must observe the rules of balanced political coverage.

For a working example, we will assume there are four candidates for

Representation of the People Act 1983. Section 30

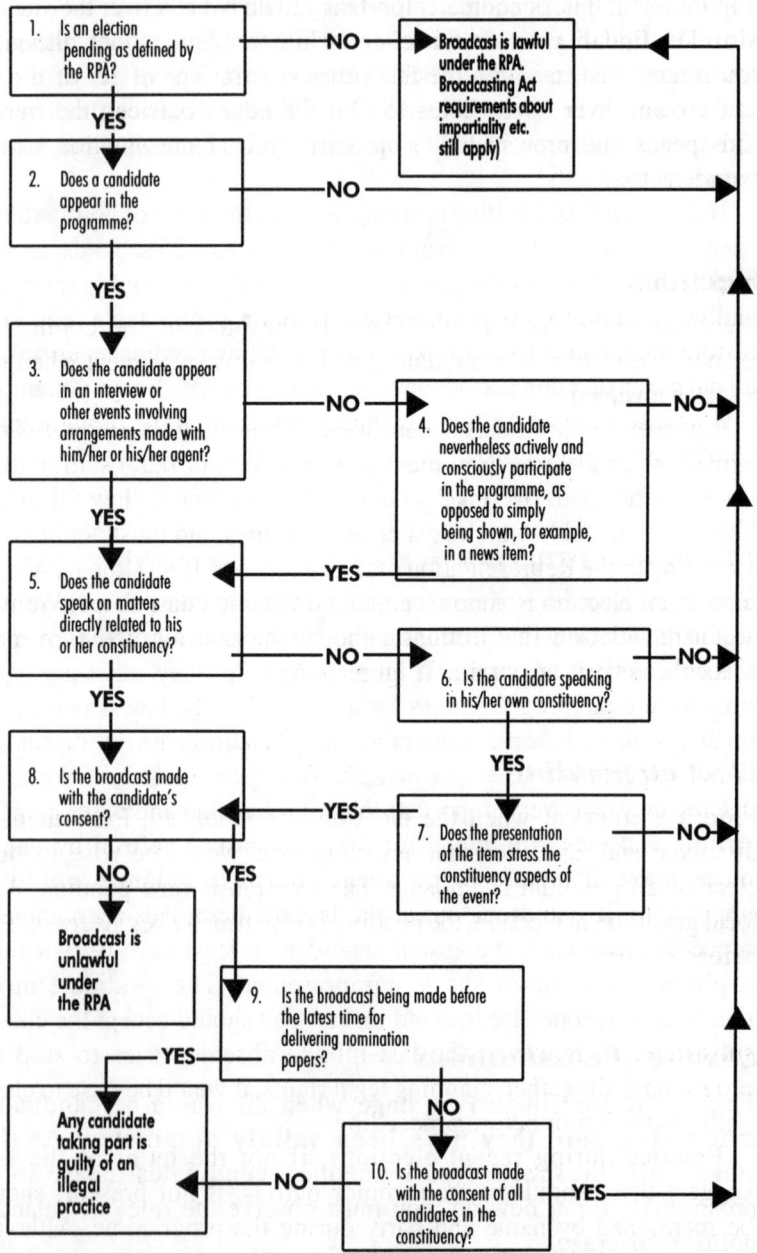

Figure 14.6 A flow diagram to illustrate the workings of the Representation of the Peoples Act. *Courtesy: Radio Authority*

the fictional constituency of Blanktown West. From the close of nominations, each candidate for Blanktown West must have equal airtime. 'Equal' can, of course, include none. But if you interview the Conservative candidate Michael Blue, you must give the same time to the other three – not necessarily on the same occasion, but overall. This means all airtime, including the clip recorded for news which has not yet been broadcast.

If 25 seconds of Mr Blue is broadcast after the close of nominations, even if it is recorded beforehand, you must provide 25 seconds, as near as possible, with the other three. If you do not, they could report you and you could face prosecution (although a warning and a request to restore the balance is more likely). If you allow candidates airtime at all during an election period (and there is no law which says you must), it is wise to keep an airtime log in the newsroom to be brought up to date after every bulletin.

Discussion programmes

You may have the idea of getting all four candidates round a studio table for a live discussion in this period. On the face of it, this is fine. But take care. If all four turn up, they must get equal time during the programme as far as possible. The law is reasonable on this point, and the presenter or journalist chairing the live discussion is not expected to use a stopwatch. But there must be no glaring discrepancy. It is very important that all the main candidates agree in writing that they will attend for the broadcast. A refusal by one or more make it unsafe to go ahead, because balance would be impossible. If one drops out at the last moment, it is reasonable to proceed, mentioning the absent candidate at least once or twice and explaining why he or she is unrepresented. The candidate might nominate someone else to stand in, and you should accept the chosen substitute. If, however, the last-minute absentee tries to stop the programme altogether, claiming legal rights, it would be wise to check with your solicitor before proceeding.

Practice during recent elections, if not the letter of the law, suggest that candidates from minor parties, if not present, should be mentioned by name and party during the programme. Although the person chairing the discussion should be impartial, that does not prevent the policies of absent candidates being put forward for discussion around the table.

Polling day

The poll opens in a General Election at 7 a.m. and ends at 10 p.m. Local elections start an hour later and finish an hour earlier. During that time, you must not broadcast any political propaganda at all, even if balanced between all candidates in a constituency.

News reports from 7 a.m. must keep to the basic facts that the polls have opened, that it is a sunny day (or otherwise), that the turnout is predicted to be heavy, and other non-political issues. From 10 p.m. that night, all special restrictions end. But watch that no candidate (in an excess of enthusiasm) says anything about one of the others which could be libellous. The law of libel is not suspended in an election!

Commentaries

The commentary is the broadcaster's chance to paint pictures for the listener. In most cases, the event itself will be a 'diary' one, which will be known about in advance, and we will discuss that here. There is another type of commentary, though – the completely unexpected moment when a news story breaks before your eyes and you have a microphone. As the rioters advance up the street, or as you watch an aircraft dive into the ground, you must literally make up what you say as you go along. There are very few pieces of advice which will come in useful then, except keep talking.

Planning

If you are to commentate at a major event, read all you can in advance. If the Queen is scheduled to meet the Sea Scouts, know the name of their commanding officer. If she will be greeted by the Lord Lieutenant of the county, make sure you know not merely his name but also why he received the DSO in 1944. It may come in handy. It is no accident that, during great national events, the commentators always have something to say. It is rare for a hold-up to occur with Coronations and other ceremonial occasions, but when one does happen, you discover just how much research the commentator has done. Much of your research will never be heard, but you will be comforted, on the day, that you have a reservoir of material which you will have reduced, naturally, into easily read notes in front of you.

Also make sure, by a visit in advance, that you will see what is going on! It will be very embarrassing to admit that your view has been blocked by a new bandstand which was put up overnight. Speak at length with the organisers. Make sure they know you will be there on the day and why.

Mood

Great occasions can be happy or sad, and it is up to the radio commentator to convey the general emotion by tone or voice. Describing the Lord Mayor's Show is not the same as describing a Remembrance Day ceremony. Be sensitive about the type of event you are covering. Nobody wants you to be a ham actor, but there are shades of emotion which you should properly use to reflect the atmosphere of an occasion.

Style and content

What you say will depend on the opportunities you are given. It may be that you are called on to provide several two-minute pieces into another programme. There is no time, then, for long reminiscences about historical details. On the other hand, you could be carrying the programme for much longer. Then more detail is essential.

Whatever else you leave out, do not forget to describe the clothing of female royalty in as much detail as you reasonably can. Many listeners are fascinated by what colours the princess has chosen for her spring collection. If male royalty wears anything other than the usual lounge suit (maybe a kilt?), then of course that should be mentioned too.

Silence, please . . .

When you are facing a microphone which is callously live for a long period, you may feel a temptation to fill every second. Resist it. However golden your tone, the listener would like a rest from them now and then. Remember that the sounds of the day itself are also available to tell their own story. Pause for a few seconds as the prince gets out of the car; let the sound of the platoon coming smartly to attention speak for itself. Your words are no substitute for the unmistakable 'thwack' of dozens of army boots all hitting the ground at precisely the same moment. If you provide the frame, the listener will be able to see the picture.

Sport

The essence of a successful sports programme is simple – supplying a fast, accurate and instant service of information. A whole book could be written about sports reporting and presenting, but here are a few hints and tips.

Match reports

Match reports are a bonus, and coverage of major events such as league soccer are governed by national contracts. The listener wants to know instantly that a goal has been scored and by whom. This is the crucial news. A reporter can add more details a few minutes later.

The main difference between TV and radio sports reporting is that on radio you are the link, whereas on TV you are the missing link. In other words, the audience can turn the voice off on TV and still follow what is going on. On radio, you are the only link with the action. The general rule for match reports and previews is to keep your pieces simple and factual. Over-elaboration confuses the listener. Avoid the over-used sporting clichés which have grown over the years.

The sports diary

The effective use of a diary is one of the most important factors in running a successful sports desk. All the match fixtures should be entered of course, but more importantly, notes should be made of follow-up

They've sprung the offside trap	He buried the cross from six yards
The goalkeeper hasn't been getting his knees dirty	He hit the ball well wide of the post
A classic match of two halves	His telescopic sight needs urgent repair
The strikers have been firing blanks all day	He headed it nowhere in particular
The visitors' defence pressed the self-destruct button	The manager must have wished he'd stayed in bed
The goalkeeper has so little to do, he is in danger of frostbite	He's going to take an early bath
He slammed the ball into the back of the net	

Figure 14.7 Well-worn sporting cliches to be avoided

stories. For example, on the first of the month you ran a story with a local team manager saying Smith is out of action for three weeks with a hamstring injury. Then, immediately, you enter the story for the 21st and check with the manager again. Not only will that show the manager that you are on top of matters, but it will also create a similar impression with the listener.

Daily sports bulletins

A successful radio sports operation's credibility is also dependent on the quality of the daily sports bulletins as well as match reports on a Saturday afternoon. These reports should be authoritative and informative. The guidelines to writing sports copy are exactly the same as for news. The key to success is to establish good relations with your contacts such as football manager or rugby coaches. To fill a sports bulletin, you have to begin from nothing. Unlike the newsdesk, you cannot rely on check calls to the emergency services, although you can establish a 'round' of calls to your club contacts.

There are three important things to remember when dealing with sports people. Firstly, be courteous. Secondly, be certain of your facts (football managers have been known to walk away from interviewers who have asked 'So who are you playing tomorrow?'). Thirdly, avoid too much speculation, however tempting.

15

The future of radio news

The future of radio news is assured. There will always be an appetite for local news. Over the next few years, there will be more local radio stations which will need local news and therefore more jobs for journalists. It is a genuine growth industry. In the commercial sector particularly, audiences also seem to be continuing to grow with the increasing choice of radio stations, which is good news for advertisers.

However, there will continue to be changes in the ways journalists work and the ways in which a newsroom works. They will operate with fewer people and those people will be required to have the all-round skills of the experienced broadcaster. It is still an exciting and challenging time to be involved in local radio news.

Ways in which news is presented on the radio will continue to evolve. Although there will always be a place for the 'tell it straight' style of radio journalism, we will see even greater emphasis on production and presentation values in the eternal quest to attract and keep audiences in a highly competitive, push-button age. Content, too, will evolve with editorial agendas for local stations clearly reflecting the values and using the language of the demographic group at which the station is aimed.

The technical revolution will continue. More newsrooms will become computerised and tape recorders and cart machines will become antique. The aim is for a tape-free and paper-free newsroom. News bulletins will be written, compiled and timed on-screen. Audio will be stored on hard disk. The news presenter will sit in front of a computer screen to deliver the bulletin, reading the script and cues off screen and touching the screen to activate audio cuts and clips. Experiments are taking place to construct the 'virtual' news bulletin which may be useful in providing stations with few resources with ways of being cost-effective and extending their news output. However, judgements still need to be made by people and the new technology which is being developed to rotate news stories automatically across a morning's news bulletins may be going a little too far.

As well as the newsroom, the reporter on the ground will become increasingly involved in the technical revolution. More use will be made of digital equipment for recording audio and interviews which will improve technical quality. The equipment will become even smaller and therefore more portable. The speed of filing stories back to base will improve with the development of ISDN lines and the mobile phone networks to say nothing of the portable computers which can be used for on-line filing of copy.

Everything is geared to allowing reporters and newsdesk journalists to do their jobs quicker and more efficiently, leaving more time to follow up other stories. Productivity will increase because the new technology is seen as a 'liberator'. The good old-fashioned radio may well even be replaced with the development of Digital Audio Broadcasting (DAB) over the next few years where large numbers of CD quality radio stations will be transmitted without any interference.

The early 1990s have seen a turbulent time in the ownership and management of local radio stations in the commercial sector, with many smaller stations now owned by large groups. These groups bring more resources but sometimes network what used to be local programming, although local news is seen as an important component in the local output, in general, protected from being absorbed into networks.

With commercial radio's profitability and success in attracting audiences and advertisers, ownership of stations and groups will continue to change with more take-overs and acquisitions. As the government allows greater deregulation, we are likely to see more local radio stations owned by local newspaper groups and also establishing links with local cable television. There is a natural synergy between these three media and there is no doubt they can work together to mutual advantage.

With all the technical and operational changes, it is even more important to remember the basic tools and techniques of radio journalism. There will always be a need for bright young talent in the industry which brings those two most important qualities – enthusiasm and ideas. It is vital to keep these people within local radio and not use local stations as simply a stepping stone to national radio and television. Local radio can be rewarding in itself. People will only stay, though, if radio continues to be exciting, with all the job satisfaction anyone could need.

However, we must guard against one of the biggest dangers of all, especially with the increasing use of news technology. There could be a tendency to think of news as that which simply appears on the screen or the printer.

Never forget that real news is what you go out and find through your own efforts.

GLOSSARY

Actuality: Usually used in the BBC to denote a recording of someone speaking, or of an event

Ad: Advertisement or commercial

Ad lib: Speaking without a script

Aircheck: A recording of a broadcaster or programme. Sometimes used for demonstration purposes

AM: Amplitude modulation, the abbreviation for broadcasts on medium wave

Anchor: Person acting as main presenter of a programme

Angle: The varying way in which a news story can be told from different points of view

Archive: A file of old stories for reference, either in copy form, audio form or both

Atmos: Atmosphere. Impression of location created by evocative background sounds. *See also* Wildtrack

Audio: Literally any sound, but frequently used in radio, especially commercial radio, to mean the same as actuality

Back anno: Back announcement after audio to give extra information

Balancing unit: *See* TBU

Barter: A way for paying for a programme or feature in commercial radio by exchanging a fee for airtime. IRN Newslink organises on a barter basis

Basys: Trade name. One of the most popular newsroom computers

Bed: A short piece of music over which information, news or headlines are read

Bi-media: Used in the BBC to indicate working both for television and radio

Break: Pause in programme for commercials or news

Bulk eraser: A device which generates a powerful magnetic field to erase tape

Cans: Slang for headphones

Cartridge ('cart'): An endless loop of tape enclosed in a plastic case. Used for short audio items including news cuts, commercials and jingles

Catchline: A one-word name used to identify a story. *See also* Slug

Check calls: Routine phone calls from a newsroom to the emergency services

Chinograph: A special soft yellow or white pencil used to mark a point on tape for editing purposes

Clean feed: The programme output in which a remote contributor hears all the elements apart from his or her own

Clean tape: Tape which is either new or has had previous recordings erased

Clip: Usually used in the BBC to denote a piece of news audio

Contra: Trade exchange in commercial radio where goods and services are traded for advertising airtime

Copy: Written material ready for broadcasting

Copy story: A news story without audio

cps: Centimetres per second (tape speed)

CRCA: Commercial Radio Companies Association. The trade body to which most commercial radio stations belong

Cue (1): The start point on a recording

Cue (2): The start signal to a live speaker

Cue (3): The written introduction to a piece of audio

Cut: Usually used in commercial radio to denote a piece of news audio

D-cart: Trade name. A popular hard disk newsroom system

DAB: Digital audio broadcasting. New technology enabling large numbers of stations to broadcast to a certain area in CD quality without interference

DAT: Digital audio tape. High quality recording on digital tape enclosed in a small plastic box smaller than a cassette

DAVE: Digital audio visual editing. A portable digital recorder and editing device

Delay: A device which inserts a time delay between studio and transmitter usually used to censor profanities and other undesirable material during live phone-in programmes

Demo tape: A recording of a broadcaster or would-be broadcaster, usually on cassette, sent with a job application

Demographics: The categorisation of audience by age, sex and social group used in audience research

Dirty tape: Tape which has not been fully erased. If a dirty cartridge is used for another recording, the previous signal will still be heard in the background

DJ: Disc jockey

Dolby: System for reducing audio noise and improving high frequency response, used especially on recording equipment

Double ender: Short length of audio cable with a jack plug on each end used to connect pieces of equipment or jacks on a jackfield

Dubbing: Copying a recording, either onto another tape or onto computer disk

Editing: Changing a recording after it has been made, usually by removing part of it either physically on tape or digitally on computer

Equalisation (EQ): Changing the frequency response of a device usually a microphone. A voice may be made deeper or crisper by equalisation, but EQ controls should only be adjusted by the experienced

Fire: To start a piece of audio, either on tape or on computer

Flag: A computer setting to alert the user to pre-arranged search criteria

Fluff: Mistake

FM: Frequency modulation. The abbreviation for broadcasts on VHF

FX: abbreviation for sound effects

GTS: Greenwich time signal, or the 'pips'

Gain control: Volume control

Gate: A self-imposed deadline beyond which no material can be accepted for broadcast, usually five minutes before a bulletin to allow for preparation

GNS: General News Service, the BBC's internal news agency supplying news material to local radio and other sources

Hard disk: The area of a computer permanently storing material for instant recall and editing

ID: Station identification or ident

ILR: Independent local radio now usually known as commercial radio

Insert: A piece of audio in the middle of a report

Intro: The introduction to a recorded report

ips: Inches per second (tape speed)

IR: Independent radio now usually known as commercial radio

IRN: Independent radio news, commercial radio's biggest national news agency

ISDN: Integrated services digital network. High quality dial-up telephone landlines which can be used for broadcast purposes, usually on a temporary basis

Jingle: Short piece of recorded music played to identify a station

Kicker: Lighthearted story at the end of a news bulletin

Landline: A special cable link which can carry sound at full bandwidth for broadcast purposes, usually used for linking permanent sites

Leader: Transparent or coloured tape which leads up to the start of a recorded item

Logger (1): A slow-speed recording of a radio station's output made for regulatory and reference purposes

Logger (2): A master recording made of the satellite or landline feed from a national news supplier for newsroom reference use

Marantz: Trade name of a popular cassette recorder

NAB: National Association of Broadcasters (US)

Nab centre: A circular device clipped into the centre of a tape spool and fitted over the spindle of an open-reel tape recorder

Newsbooth: Small studio where news bulletins are presented on air

Newslink: The advertisement played on commercial radio next to peak time news bulletins by which local stations pay for the national news agency IRN

Newstar: Trade name of a popular newsroom computer system

OB: Outside broadcast

Open reel: Tape recorder with two reels, also known as a reel-to-reel recorder

Optimod: Trade name for popular transmitter processing device

Opting: The practice of leaving or joining a network for programmes

P as B: Usually used in the BBC to mean programme as broadcast

P as R: Usually used in the BBC to mean programme as recorded

PA (1): Press Association

PA (2): Public address system

Package: Usually used in the BBC to denote a broadcast report consisting of a journalist's voice plus at least one insert of audio

Popping: The break-up of signal from a microphone caused by explosive consonants when speaking too close

Pot: Potentiometer. Still used in the BBC, but now being replaced by faders. The volume control of a sound source used for setting its level

Pot point: A suitable moment, such as the end of a sentence, in which a piece of audio can be stopped early if required

PPM: Peak programme meter. A device with scale which measures sound levels (more technically, the measurement of peak values of broadcast output)

Prefade: Listening to an item before playing it on air, usually used to check levels

Promo: An on-air (and usually pre-recorded) promotion for a forthcoming programme, item, or event

Q and A: Question-and-answer where a reporter is quizzed by a presenter. Can also mean an interview. *See also* Two-way

RAB: The Radio Advertising Bureau. The organisation which publicises the benefits of commercial radio in general to advertisers

Racks: The room in a radio station containing engineering equipment

RAJAR: Radio Audience Joint Research. The agreed method of audience measurement between commercial radio and the BBC

Remote studio: A small studio, usually unstaffed, connected to a main studio centre by landline, ISDN or radio link

Rip 'n' read: News bulletin copy sent from central newsroom intended for instant reading on air without rewriting

ROT: Record off transmission. Literally, a recording of the broadcast via a radio set. Sometimes used, less accurately, to mean any recording of studio output

RPA: The Representation of the Peoples Act which governs elections and the reporting of them

RSL: Restricted Service Licence. The Radio Authority grants RSL licences to groups for one month to broadcast over a small area of a few miles for a special event or as a trial service for a new permanent licence

Running Order: List of items within a programme, giving titles and durations

RX: Recording

Sadie: Trade name for popular studio on-screen digital editor, mainly used for production purposes more than news

Segue: The following of one item immediately on the other without interruption or pause

Self-op: The process of self-operation of a studio control desk by a journalist or presenter

Slug: Short identifying name given to a news story on a computer or a script

Snap: A newsflash

Soundbite: Used in both BBC and commercial stations to describe an audio or actuality cut with a short (less than 30 second) excerpt of an interview

Splicing: The process of cutting and rejoining tape for editing purposes

Splicing tape: A specialised sticky tape designed for editing

Stab: A short, emphatic jingle or ident

Sweep: A period of time when audience research is being carried out

Talkback: Intercom device for talking to people in other studios or other parts of the radio station

TBU: Telephone Balancing Unit. A piece of equipment used to match the studio output with an incoming telephone line for recording or live transmission

Teasers: Short and intriguing headlines to promote a forthcoming programme or item

Topline: The first line in a copy story or cue

Traffic: Used in commercial radio to denote the department of the station which schedules commercials for transmission

Trails: A short promotion for a forthcoming programme or item

Two-way: Usually used in the BBC to mean a discussion or interview between studios remote from each other. Frequently used to mean a reporter questioned on air about a story

TX: Transmission

Uher: Trade name for a popular portable tape recorder

UHF: Ultra high frequency

Umbrella: A single story incorporating a number of similar items under one banner

Voicebank: The telephone system used by emergency services to distribute information on incidents to the media

Voicer: A news story explained by a reporter within a bulletin (sometimes called a voice piece in the BBC)

Vox pop: Vox populi. Latin meaning 'voice of the people'. A series of comments on a single issue gathered at random from members of the public and edited into a sequence

VU meter: Volume unit meter. A device to measure sound levels. It is less common in professional use than the PPM Meter being more inaccurate at some frequencies

Waveform: The system used by a computer to display a recorded sound for editing purposes on screen

Wildtrack: Background noise recorded on location for later use in wraps and packages

Windshield: A foam cover for a microphone which helps reduce noise and popping

Wire services: News agencies

Wipe: To erase tape

Wrap: Usually used in commercial radio to denote a broadcast report consisting of a journalist's voice plus at least one insert of audio

Index